Bill Wallace of China

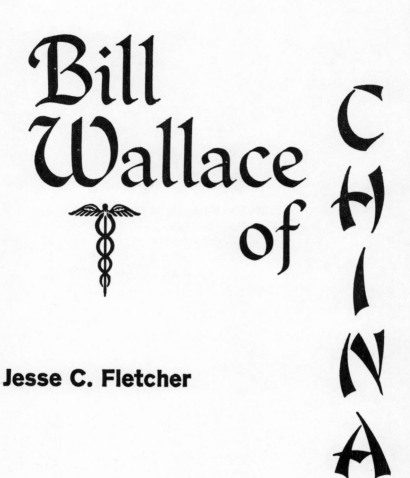

Bill Wallace of China

Jesse C. Fletcher

BROADMAN PRESS
Nashville, Tennessee

Eighth Printing

Library of Congress Catalog Card Number: 63-17522

Printed in the United States of America

3.5MH6513

To Dorothy, Scott, and Melissa
and
to the medical missionaries around the world
whose heritage has been enriched by the life of
Bill Wallace

Contents

Preface

The name William L. Wallace will live through the years
to come. His service as a medical missionary in China brought
healing and relief to countless people. His character as a Christian
man was a strong influence in his city. The Stout Memorial Hospital
he served was regarded as one of the major medical institutions of
South China.

When the Communists were about to take charge of China, the
missionaries were asked to make their own decisions concerning
evacuating or staying longer. Dr. Wallace replied, "I will stay as
long as I can do any good."

He sealed his Christian testimony with his life's blood. He ministered to all people alike, even after the Communists took charge.
His imprisonment and his death after fifty-three days of suffering
are told in this book.

The author has caught the spirit of the missionary and has identified with him in purpose and idealism. With rare insight the book
tells the story of a noble life dedicated to the service of God and his
fellow man.

Those who read this book will understand the spirit which char-
acterizes the author as he gives counsel and guidance to an ever-
increasing number of missionary candidates in preparation for
service abroad.

It is my prayer that this splendid volume may lead all who read
it into a deeper dedication and to a clearer awareness of the will of
Christ for their lives.

BAKER J. CAUTHEN
Executive Secretary
Foreign Mission Board
Southern Baptist Convention

Prologue

This is the story of an ordinary man, who, in the providence of God, lived an extraordinary life. Bill Wallace served as a medical missionary in China during seventeen of the most turbulent years of the ancient kingdom's history. The doctor, who was reared in Knoxville, Tennessee, became a legend among the people he served. At the peak of his ministry, he was called upon to seal his Christian witness with his life. In February, 1951, he died—a martyr for Christ—in a Communist prison cell.

The Wallace story has waited twelve years to be told. Except for scraps of information in brief articles in various publications, the incredible, inspiring facts of his life are unknown. Several reasons are evident. Bill Wallace seldom spoke of his experiences, wrote almost nothing, and was never of a nature to attract attention to himself. Too, he died behind the Bamboo Curtain, and so many of the people who really know the story are not free to tell it. And, of course, the scene of his labors and fabled acts of heroism is no longer accessible.

Ordinarily, twelve years such as those of the fast-moving fifties and sixties would be enough to swallow the memory of the man who perished in such a distant and (so far as the world goes) uncelebrated place. But his has not been the case; his memory has refused to die. Preachers, searching for apt illustrations, have reached again and again into the meager little reservoir of known facts about the martyred doctor, and thus few Baptists have failed to hear his name, though they know little about the man. Missionaries and mission board representatives, inspired by his life, have challenged a complacent generation in place after place with the story of his discipleship. And, every now and then, a new missionary appointee going to serve his Lord on a foreign field will

1

speak of a resolve planted in his mind and heart by the life and death of Bill Wallace.

Dr. M. Theron Rankin, late executive secretary of the Southern Baptist Foreign Mission Board, said, "The Communists thought they were rid of him, but instead they have immortalized him." They immortalized him in the lives of those who knew him, those who experienced the mercies of his great heart and skilled hands, and those who heard the story of witness unto death. This book is not capable of adding to such experiential canonization. But because of the impact his life has had on these people, perhaps the whole story (as sketchy as it must be) will enable still others to catch the spirit of adventuresome discipleship and disciplined commitment that characterized his life.

That goal has dictated the form of this biography—narrative rather than critical—in order that the man might be seen in action and not in retrospect. The method or form has caused the author to use freely conjecture, but never apart from fact, known impressions, or reliable reports.

This, to the best of my ability and to the limit of my research, is the Bill Wallace story.

I would like to express my deep gratitude to the following persons, without whose help this task could not have been accomplished: Mrs. Robert Beddoe, Miss Mary Christian, Miss Nelle Davidson, Miss Marilyn Fairfax, Dr. and Mrs. Ed Galloway, Miss Ione Gray, Miss Genevieve Greer, Miss Everley Hayes, Dr. and Mrs. Eugene Hill, Dr. Dewey Peters, Mrs. M. Theron Rankin (now deceased), Dr. Sam Rankin, Miss Nell Stanley, Mrs. Roy Starmer, Mr. and Mrs. Sydney Stegall, Mrs. Gene Newton West, and Miss Lucy Wright.

The Single Stream

There was almost no breeze. In the stillness it seemed that time was suspended, as indeed it was for Bill Wallace. Inside the garage where he sat, the shadows offered some relief from the brilliant sunshine which reached in from the opened doors to expose a partially dismantled Ford, a grimy but orderly workbench, an assortment of oil-smeared wrenches, and a small New Testament open on the bench.

The physician's seventeen-year-old son, whose main claim to fame was his phenomenal mechanical skill, was working diligently when his moment of destiny seized him. The first assault slowed him; the second caused a mistake; the third stopped him.

Laying aside his wrench, he picked up his New Testament as if it could offer an answer for the demanding question that without warning had taken command of his consciousness. What should he do with his life? No, that was not quite accurate. He was not sure the question was so self-determinative. Better, what would God have him do with his life?

An intruder, had there been one (and anybody would have been one in the moment), would not, could not have realized that forces at work in this young man on this hot, still, uninspiring afternoon would forever decide his life's course. Neither the place nor props, not even the slouching figure of the lean, sandy-haired youth, would have revealed it; but that is what was happening.

Can the "heavenly vision" be so mundane? Can God's Holy Spirit grasp men and set them apart for special tasks in such ordinary circumstances? Well, it was, and he did; and it happened right there in that garage.

Apart from any previous reference to anything remotely akin to this, the young mechanic-to-be, trade school bound, decided that

3

day, in that moment, in that place, that God was calling *him* to be a medical missionary in a place that He would some day reveal.

His one immediate act of response—scrawling in the grease-stained New Testament his purpose and then subsequently handing the New Testament to his sister—in no way revealed the depth of the experience or the dynamic nature of his call; but it was his way. He always understated things.

The date was July 5, 1925. This was the beginning, the fountainhead of a man's destiny. Its significance became more apparent when it merged with another seemingly unimportant event, nine years later and half a world away.

Two hundred miles up China's West River lies the ancient city of Wuchow. There, in the fall of 1934, the cry of a people's suffering was distinctly heard and answered from the Stout Memorial Hospital, a five-story stone monument to the effective compassion of the Christ in dedicated men's hearts. In a tiny office overlooking the treaty-port city which straddled the confluence of the West and Fu Rivers, the balding, precise superintendent, Dr. Robert E. Beddoe, was trying his best to communicate that cry.

The office was hot. Reams of correspondence, rows of books, stacks of files, and an oversized old desk filled it to the point of suffocation. On the desk rested a service-weary old typewriter. Wiping the sweat from his starched collar with an already soaked handkerchief, the doctor, who had given the best years of his life to the nurturing of this Southern Baptist outpost of mercy, paused for a moment from his furious typing—he referred to himself as China's fastest two-fingered typist—and stared out the one small window. Lazy herons floated on thermals over the West River, casually surveying the activity below. Dr. Beddoe noted that the river traffic was unusually heavy, probably due to the Generalissimo's troop movements to the West to liquidate the Communist pockets that plagued his efforts to bring China's many provinces under Nationalist Party leadership.

From the open door came familiar sounds of hospital activity, and familiar smells. The administrator sniffed the distinctive breath of his domain: antiseptics, drugs, ether, even the bleach used on the immaculate white uniforms of the attendants and nurses; all interwoven with the ever-present smells of China. He rubbed his eyes, which had for a long time been his "thorn in the flesh," and began his typing once more:

"We have a long and noble history here at the Stout Memorial Hospital, and Southern Baptists can be proud of what has been done in the name of the Lord Jesus Christ. But we are in danger of losing that position that has been so hard won, and neglecting grossly the responsibilities that are ours in this desert of suffering and heathenism. Without a surgeon, this hospital is operating in a limited capacity, and its potential as a teaching institution and an influential lighthouse for all of China is going unrealized.

"We must have another missionary doctor, a surgeon who can come in and do things I have not been able to do since my eyes gave way so many years ago. I repeat. *We must have a surgeon.*

"I appeal to you, in behalf of all the suffering which you your-self are aware of here, find us a surgeon."

Finishing with a flourish, he pulled the paper from the machine and impatiently folded it. If importunity were the answer, he would already have a hundred doctors here, and he knew the needs of South China's millions could absorb every one of them and hardly show it. Below, he could see the ever-present queue snaking out before the clinic. "O God, give us a surgeon."

The shape of the future was emerging for Bill Wallace. An ancient nation's hurt awaited only the commitment of the skilled surgeon the young man had become in obedience to his sense of God's leadership. They were synchronized in God's timing, if not in ours, and in his economy they flowed into a single stream of divine purpose that very month.

Knoxville's General Hospital had called its chief resident away from his letter writing half a dozen times before he finally finished his task. Now he addressed an envelope to the Foreign Mission Board, Southern Baptist Convention, Richmond, Virginia. He started to insert the letter, then decided to read it once more.

"My name is William L. Wallace and I am now serving as a resident in surgery at Knoxville General Hospital, Knoxville, Tennessee.

"Since my senior year in high school, I have felt God would have me to be a medical missionary, and to that end I have been preparing myself. I attended the University of Tennessee for my premedical work and received the M.D. from the University Medical School in Memphis. I did an internship here at Knoxville General and remained for a surgical residency.

"I am not sure what you desire by way of information, but I am single, twenty-six years old, and I am a member of the Broadway Baptist Church. My mother died when I was eleven and my father, also a physician, passed away two years ago. There were only two of us, and my sister, Ruth Lynn, is planning marriage.

"I must confess, I am not a good speaker nor apt as a teacher, but I do feel God can use my training as a physician. As humbly as I know how, I want to volunteer to serve as a medical missionary under our Southern Baptist Foreign Mission Board.

"I have always thought of Africa, but I will go anywhere I am needed."

As Bill read over the letter that would initiate the final step in the realization of his purpose, he was aware of once more understating things. But that is the way he was. Slowly sealing the envelope, he got up from the night nurse's desk, stuffed his stethoscope in the pocket of his white coat, and walked down the hall to the mail drop. A window at the end of the hall revealed the gray light of a new dawn.

The Southern Baptist Foreign Mission Board had been through lean days. The task of leading it to better ones fell to Dr. Charles Maddry, and it was Dr. Maddry who received the letters from Dr. Beddoe and Dr. Wallace that fall of 1934. It occurred to him they symbolized the hope that empowered his dreams. Here a letter from China—the need; here a letter from Knoxville—the man. The man and the need brought together coincidentally or purposefully? It was not a valid question in Dr. Maddry's mind; God worked that way. It was the assurance God would continue to work in such a way that gave him the courage to dream of over-coming limited finances, complacent constituents, and self-centered churches. God's purposes were greater than any barrier or discouragement he faced. But he deeply appreciated a little reassurance from time to time, and this these letters accomplished.

To himself he mused, "Dr. Wallace, meet Dr. Beddoe. You are the answer to his prayers, only you don't know it yet."

Nor could *he* be sure, the administrator reminded himself. First, he would have to investigate the young man. The issues were too important to send someone who lacked training and experience, or Christian character and commitment. Somehow (intuitively or hopefully) he felt that this man was equipped with those qualifications.

The weeks following vindicated his feeling. As answers came to his letters of inquiry about the fitness for missionary service of one William L. Wallace, a picture of the young man began to take shape.

"This young man," a family friend wrote, "is uniquely prepared for the task for which he is being considered. His father, William L. Wallace, Sr., was for many years one of the most beloved physicians in Knoxville. Dr. Wallace, Sr., and his wife, the former Elizabeth Anne George, built their home on the corner of Broadway and Silver Place. There, he practiced medicine and reared his family.

"When Bill was but eleven—a spirited, even mischievous lad, I might add—the influenza of that year took his charming mother. The father and the maternal grandmother raised the children she left.

"As I think of it now, Bill Wallace became rather shy about this time; whether the events are related or not, I am not in a position to say, but he was a good boy and very close to his father. He used to drive his father on his calls. From a very early age he was fascinated by automobiles, and he had quite a talent for mechanics. This was probably a good thing, because, while some boys achieve self-respect through sports and others in academics and still others in more social lines, Bill seemed to find his sense of worth by excelling in mechanics. He really became quite well known in his avocation. I must confess we all felt sure he would study automotive engineering or the like.

"You see, his decision to be a medical missionary came as quite a surprise to those of us who are close to the family. I mean he was quiet and held his own counsel and there was no real indication he would choose to so address himself. He was a devout lad, though, and from his conversion, he was faithful to his church. He was especially active in the boys' organization, Royal Ambassadors.

"He liked to stay in the background; in fact, he probably always will. But it is my conviction that he will be unable to remain in the background, for in his mild demeanor there is a great drawing power. I feel he is destined to render our God great service.

"After he made his decision for missions, he entered the University of Tennessee, and, despite his earlier academic record (we never thought of Bill as a scholar), he did very well. It was an early proof of his determination to prepare himself for the task God had called him to. Then he went to Memphis and medical school.

"One of the sad things, to my way of thinking, is that his father—such a wonderful man—died as Bill finished medical school and did not live to see him become the wonderful physician that the doctors who work with him at Knoxville General assure me he is. Bill has missed his father, but he has given all he has to the profession his father honored by such distinguished service for so long; and now, he has given all that his profession can mean to the cause of Christ."

This information, and more that came to substantiate it, led Dr. Maddry to feel that it was time to meet the young doctor for himself. In November he arranged a conference during a train stopover in Knoxville. He was pleased with what he found. Bill Wallace was likable, earnest, and, from all he could tell, extremely well motivated to the task of missionary service.

Dr. Maddry wrote Dr. Beddoe following that interview, the **first ray** of hope he had felt free to give the China missionary:

"I now have hopes for you in the person of a fine young man, William L. Wallace, General Hospital, Knoxville, Tennessee. He is thoroughly prepared and, from all I can gather, is a splendid young man. . . . I think he is going to be the man. . . ."

A final obstruction was yet to be passed, however, before the single stream of divine purpose was to flow its unhindered way. Bill Wallace was to be tested, to the very core of his commitment.

Dr. Dewey Peters, a long-time friend of Bill's father and soon to become a member of the American College of Surgeons, called Bill one day shortly after the interview with Dr. Maddry. He asked him if he could come by his office. Bill was excited about the conference and looked forward to it as an opportunity to talk with his former Sunday school teacher and adviser about the possibility of his appointment as a missionary.

After leaving word with the duty nurse where he might be reached in case of an emergency, he signed out and walked through the nippy winter air to Dr. Peters' office.

"Hi, William! Come in." Bill eagerly gripped the extended hand and took a seat in the well-appointed office.

He could always tell a friend of the family. To them he would always be "William." Most of his adult friends had adopted the more informal "Bill."

"You're doing a good job as chief. I'm proud I recommended you."

Bill blushed; praise always embarrassed him. "I appreciate your urging me to stay on, Dr. Peters. I hesitate to think of my limitations, had I not had this residency. But," he grinned, "it has made me hungry for more. I could become a professional student and not tire of it."

"That's a good attitude to keep, Doctor. You never get through learning in this business. No matter how pressing your load might get, don't stop studying or you will suffer, and more, your patients will suffer. Make up your mind now to practice only the best medicine throughout all your life."

Bill nodded. It was good advice and he was never to forget it.

"But I didn't call you over for a lecture, Doctor." They both

laughed. Dr. Peters paused a moment, obviously framing his
words carefully.

"I want you to consider a proposition, William. I have been
giving it a lot of thought and I feel good about it." Again he
paused, looking steadily at the slender, clean-cut features of the
young resident across from him. "I would like for you to come in
with me and share my practice. It could count as a preceptorship
toward your Boards now, and, in time, it can become a full part-
nership."

There it was. Dr. Peters did not have to tell Bill it would pay
handsomely and that prestige and unlimited opportunity were
part and parcel with it. He was far too modest to claim the
truth—that his office was practicing what he preached, "the best
medicine." Bill knew this. To a man who had been infected by
the best spirit of the medical profession, a burning zeal to wage
relentless war against the threats of disease and untimely death,
the offer was a genuine temptation. It was a young resident's
dream; it was the supreme accolade to his efforts to prepare
himself; it was also a test of his understanding of God's leadership.

For several days he prayed over the matter. He felt he owed
Dr. Peters a careful consideration. Money? That part did not in-
trigue him. As a friend said, "Dr. Wallace would be called a
strange fellow by the hustlers, bustlers, and seekers of wealth who
people the world today. They would call him stupid and imprac-
tical, for when people asked him the charge for services, he would
usually answer, 'Forget about it.' He was all charity; a sort of
mystic walking on clouds and looking for the stars. Earthly world-
lings who spent so much time figuring nickels and dimes walked
far below the plane of Dr. Wallace."[1]

Fame? It would only embarrass him. Prestige? Oh, he would
love to qualify someday as a fellow in the International College
of Surgeons, but primarily because it would mean he was a man
who could be depended on to do his best. Then whence the
temptation? It tempted him because it meant the opportunity to

---

[1]M. A. Tennien, *No Secret Is Safe Behind the Bamboo Curtain* (New York: Farrar, Straus,
and Cudahy, Inc.)

learn, to perfect, to explore the frontiers of his science, and such
would not be easy, if possible, on the mission field.

But he had lived with his orders too long to abandon them now.
God had called him and trained him for a wholly different type of
life. A few days later he returned and thanked the elder doctor for
the compliment and tried to explain his missionary ambition. He
shared his recent interview with Dr. Maddry and then added as
an afterthought and with a shy grin, "If for some reason I am
turned down, I believe you know that I will be genuinely interested." But deep in his heart he knew his destiny was now joined
with the Stout Memorial Hospital in China.

As Bill left Dr. Peters' office and started back to the hospital, he
felt a deep sense of real peace. He was grateful for the experience;
it had cleared away the last clouds. He recalled a paragraph from
a letter he had received from Dr. Beddoe in Wuchow:

"I have importuned Dr. Maddry to send out a young surgeon.
It appears that you may be the man for this job. I hope and pray
that this may be true. Your pastor writes most enthusiastically
about you. If you are the man, I pray you may come quickly.
The time is short. We must make our contribution while it is day.

"I could write for hours about this situation. I believe I could
thrill you with its possibilities. But my time is limited and I shall
not burden you further. It is a most unusual opening for one who
is on fire to glorify God in his life. I hope you are that man."

Bill silently prayed that he was that man.

The spring of 1935 passed quickly, with forms and more forms
from the Foreign Mission Board to be filled out in the rare moments of solitude allowed by his resident responsibilities. The word
came in May. If he could be in Richmond in July, he would be
examined by the Board, and if approved, he would be appointed
and could set sail for the Orient no later than September.

Dr. Beddoe was writing Bill Wallace regularly now, and in one
letter he inquired, discreetly, if Bill planned to bring a wife with
him. Bill had to laugh. Others had also inquired. Everybody said
that if he were going to throw himself away in a pagan land he
ought at least to take a wife along. But it provoked some more

serious thought also. He admired attractive women and especially witty ones, and there was one who had received the major portion of his attentions. Did he love her? He honestly did not know. Perhaps, more important, could he justify taking her to interior China? In June he attended a Baptist conference at Ridgecrest Assembly in western North Carolina and took her along. Many who saw them together speculated that the young doctor might be planning on a partner after all. But the woman herself later explained, "It was out of the question. It would have been bigamy; Bill Wallace was already married to his work."

On July 24, 1935, he went before the Southern Baptist Foreign Mission Board, which examined him in regard to his preparation, sense of calling, and commitment to the missionary endeavor. They all agreed: this young man was completely dedicated and thoroughly prepared for the task to which he believed God was calling him; they enthusiastically moved his appointment. On July 25, 1935, ten years to the month from the time he had made his garage commitment and recorded it on the back leaf of his New Testament, Dr. William L. Wallace was appointed as a medical missionary to serve in Wuchow, South China.

The single stream of divine purpose now flowed steadily East.

2

His Hand to the Plow

On September 6, 1935, Bill Wallace sailed from San Francisco Harbor. Across the mouth of San Francisco Bay, the beginnings of the great Golden Gate Bridge still hung somewhere between dream and reality.

As the deep blue waters churned in the ship's wake, Bill watched the receding California hills. A wave of nostalgia gripped him as his mind reached back to Knoxville. His throat tightened as he recalled his last Sunday there—Bill Wallace Day at Broadway Baptist Church.

The church people whom he had known so long and loved so well had responded to his appointment magnificently. An offering taken the morning he left was enough to pay his first year's salary, the salary for his language teacher for one year, his outfit and freight allowance, plus his travel expenses.

While the Foreign Mission Board would ordinarily provide this money, the people at Broadway wanted the privilege for themselves, and they sent their offering to the Board to cover these expenses. They told Bill that the missionary challenge—the Christian imperative—had never been more real to them than when this, one of their own sons, went out from them to fulfil it. After a brief sermon by the pastor, Bill was asked to speak. Speechmaking, never easy for him, was doubly hard that morning.

"As you know, I will be working at the Stout Memorial Hospital in Wuchow, South China. I'll appreciate your prayers—I deeply need them." He paused and looked down for a moment. "I really don't know what to say . . . I guess it's a good thing I'm a doctor, considering my speaking abilities." He chuckled and the audience responded kindly.

"Maybe I ought to say this, though. Many people have asked

13

me why I do not stay, with all the work there is to be done right here. I am not sure I know just what I should say to them, but I do know I'm going to China because God is leading me there."

The church was packed, and afterwards nearly two hundred of the people accompanied Bill to the station. This was the most difficult moment of all, not only because he was leaving his loved ones—his sister had married only two weeks before—but because he did not feel worthy of their praise.

The following Sunday Bill Wallace, on the steamship *President Coolidge,* heading for Wuchow, South China, recalled that sweet service held in Broadway. The memory was ringing in his heart. But he could not spend his time looking at the wake of the ship, clinging to what was behind; it was time he turned toward the bow—and the Orient. He had laid his hand to the plow. There would be no turning back.

September had not quite given way to October when the *President Coolidge* steamed into Hong Kong's mighty harbor. Brief stops at Tokyo and Shanghai had introduced Bill to the Orient, but he found that no sight was quite like that of the bustling British colony—the fabulous, mysterious, and gaudily decorated door to the ancient Chinese kingdom.

A riot of sight, sound, and smell greeted him. Majestic views, colorful sampans, fabulous buildings, squalid filth, and suffering constituted the multisplendored scene. People, masses of people, were everywhere. Bill was not the first missionary to be speechless and yet full of things he wanted to say.

The awed young missionary leaned over the rail, as the SS *Coolidge* came to its anchorage, and tried to realize he was at the gateway of the land to which he had given his life. Even without its Manchurian provinces, which had been taken in 1932 by Japan, China was as large as the United States and boasted a population of one-fourth of all the world's people. Here was a nation which had seen the rise and fall of the great historic civilizations. And here was the scene of some of the most dramatic and heroic missionary service in the history of Christian expansion.

"You are joining quite a heritage, you know." It was an older missionary, returning for another denomination, who spoke. Bill nodded, wondering if the missionary sensed the thoughts which raced through his mind. The older man went on: "Missionaries came to this land as far back as the eighth century, but the land swallowed them up and buried them in its fathomless antiquity. Roman Catholics made missionary efforts all through the four-teenth and fifteenth centuries, but the Manchus made Christianity illegal in 1724 and all but obliterated what little had been accom-plished."

The wide-eyed young doctor was unconsciously splicing the smells and sights before his eyes with the sound track of the mis-sionary narrator beside him.

"You've heard of Robert Morrison, of course. We consider him the father of Protestant missions in China. He was an Englishman, taking his inspiration from one of your Baptists, William Carey. He transcended all barriers before him to pave the way for us and the gospel into this ancient civilization.

"They say it was Morrison, who in reply to the cynical state-ment, 'So then you really expect to make an impression on the idolatry of a great Chinese empire?' answered, 'No sir. I expect God will!' "

Below them a sampan maneuvered alongside. It was full of boys wanting to dive for coins. The missionary glanced down but con-tinued:

"Following Morrison, others came to the Orient under the same conviction. They paid a big price. It is said that in those early days the average missionary life was only seven years after their arrival here. During the first half-century only one attained the ripe old age of forty. As a medical man you are entering into a particularly noble heritage. It was just a hundred years ago that Dr. Peter Parker, a Congregationalist, came to begin medical missions in China. Many historians say that he opened China at the point of a lancet."

Bill took it all in. This was the land of the Boxer Rebellion of 1900, when hundreds of Protestant missionaries and thousands of Chinese Christians were put to death by a Chinese reactionary regime. Many had refused pardon at the price of renouncing their Saviour, choosing to seal the testimony of their faith with their blood. Now people thought that those days were behind: that men and women would never again have to lay down their lives for their faith. This was the civilized twentieth century.

Missionaries from all over China were at the docks when the boat arrived. With the coming of Bill's group, the Baptists were welcoming their first reinforcements in more than a decade. Their joy was unbounded. The hope for advance was incarnated in this awe-stricken group of new missionaries. Among those who gathered to welcome them was one particularly interested in the arrival of the medical missionary, Dr. William L. Wallace. For Dr. R. E. Beddoe, director of the Stout Memorial Hospital in Wuchow, this day marked the answer to his prayers for help. Another doctor was arriving; a man to meet never-ending suffering with skilled hands, trained eyes, and a heart that belonged to Jesus Christ. How he had longed for this moment!

The next afternoon Bill Wallace and Dr. Beddoe boarded the West River steamer bound inland for Wuchow. Dr. Beddoe wanted to introduce Bill to the hospital before the new missionary returned to Canton for his year of language study. The boat was loaded to capacity with four classes of passengers and an infinite variety of cargo. Granted normal conditions, it took twenty-four hours to steam across the bay to West River and up its wide green waters to Wuchow. The difficult 220-mile trip was often beset by floods, river pirates, and hijacking.

Still stunned by the newness of it all, Bill Wallace avidly devoured the river sights as his excited new supervisor pointed them out. The green banks began to grow hilly as the steamer moved inland and the changing scene became breath-taking and intriguing. Every few miles a village clung to the water's edge. Bill watched coolies, with their wide tentlike straw hats, working in the fields, treading a crude water pump, or pulling a boat. Near the villages, naked children played at the river's edge and women washed their clothes with the aid of paddles.

Dr. Beddoe pointed out one of the typical villages with houses of mud walls and thatched roofs. "Their floors are mere pounded earth. Those windows are a lattice of wood covered with paper, as glass is scarce and costly. As you can see, their outbuildings are made of woven bamboo. You will find that wood is a precious commodity here and the farmers use it sparingly for roof beams, farm implements, furniture, and coffins."

In the courtyards of the tiny homes Bill could see women spinning and mending and preparing food. He saw old people sitting in the sun, children playing, pigs rooting, and chickens scratching in search of stray bits of food. He saw poverty, filth, and disease; but he also saw people. His heart warmed to them. Very soon now he would call them his people and China his home.

Shortly after lunch the second day, the steamer passed through a high gorge. Dr. Beddoe said, "This gorge is a beautiful sight about sundown; you can see then a kaleidoscope of colors. But don't let its beauty fool you. It can cause a great deal of woe in Wuchow. You see, after the rains come, the West River and the Fu River, which comes into the West River at Wuchow, expel so much water it starts backing up at these gorges. Like a great big bottleneck it backs it right up into our front yard. You will see what I mean before many months have passed."

Moments later Dr. Beddoe pointed excitedly to a high hill where a Chinese pagoda stood starkly outlined against fleecy white clouds. Within the next instant the buildings of Wuchow appeared and Bill Wallace spied his new home.

Wuchow was built from the edge of the river up the side of encircling hills. Beginning on the north bank of the West River, the city extended along the bank to the confluence of the smaller Fu River and then up the northeast side of the Fu. The mouth of the Fu was congested with sampans, junks, and barges. Many of them were nothing more than houseboats, and laundry hung from boat to boat.

As the river steamer maneuvered to dock, Dr. Beddoe grabbed Bill by the arm and called his attention to a large five-story building halfway up a high hill. Bill had visualized it many times in his mind's eye: the Stout Memorial Hospital.

A greeting in English drew Bill's attention to the dock. There stood the missionaries of the Wuchow station surrounded by a ring of giggling young Chinese nurses in crisp, white uniforms. He already knew the missionaries' names. He now tried to pick them out from their pictures he had seen in the *Missionary Album*. He identified the tall Texan, Rex Ray, and Mrs. Ray. Then he saw the veteran Molly McMinn, who was in her last term of a long and illustrious career. Watching Dr. Beddoe's spirited waving, he did not have to guess which one was Mrs. Beddoe. Soon they were on the dock and the warm, affectionate missionaries immediately took the winsome young doctor to their hearts.

As the welcoming procession hustled Bill through customs and then up the streets toward the hospital, he tried to keep his mind on the things his fellow missionaries were saying and, at the same time, take in the scene about him. They dodged precariously loaded handcarts bumping along on crude wheels. Coolies doing little quick steps down the street balanced baskets full of poultry.

Bill heard the squeal of pigs and smelled the odor of fish and meat for sale on the open market. He side-stepped rickshas and careening cyclists and gaped at great red paper lanterns strung in front of every shop and across the streets. There was too much to see. Then he stood at the entrance of the famous Stout Memorial Hospital.

The great five-story building, with its surrounding wall and two-story clinic, was an imposing and unexpected sight in the interior of China. Passing through the clinic arcade, Bill saw a beautiful lawn sloping up green terraces to the high steps of the hospital itself. There the entire staff stood ready to greet their long-prayed-for doctor.

It was evening before he had a chance to be alone. He walked through the gardens that surrounded the bungalows beside the hospital and from the top terrace looked out across the city of Wuchow to the tranquil West River shimmering in the twilight. The remains of a magnificent sunset languished on the hills beyond. As the cool evening breeze caressed his face, he thanked God for the opportunity that was to be his.

His introduction to Wuchow lasted two weeks. At first he felt a bit out-of-pocket, but on the fourth day he performed emergency surgery, and the hospital was his. The nurses who had attended talked excitedly of the new doctor's skill and technique. The interns and residents vied for an opportunity to assist or just watch in the next surgery, which was scheduled two days later. His fellow missionaries nodded to one another with a silent "He'll do."

Then it was time to go to Canton and begin language studies. Dr. Beddoe assured Bill he could continue language study the next year at Wuchow. Bill bade his new colleagues farewell, and, after promising to come for Christmas, boarded the ferry to Canton.

Bill did not know that after he had gone, Dr. Beddoe sat down to record his impressions of the new doctor. A firm, dedicated man, whose greatest gift was organization and efficient administration, Dr. Beddoe had been inclined to emphasize those aspects of the hospital while he was showing his new colleague around. He had noticed, somewhat to his dismay, that Bill was more interested in the medical aspects than the organizational aspects. After noting his lack of interest in administrative details, Beddoe decided that Bill was not executive material. He wrote Dr. Maddry:

"Dr. Wallace has been here and I have observed him carefully. He is a very fine boy and I believe will eventually develop into a good man for this work. I doubt, however, that he will acquire the executive ability necessary to manage this hospital, but this, if true, may prove a blessing since he can concentrate on the medical side of the work.

"I feel that he will have difficulty with the language. I say this because he has no musical ear—which is necessary to hear Chinese inflection and properly reproduce what he hears.

"However, Wallace has made a good impression on the Chinese people—which is the most important thing a new missionary can do. Our workers have fallen for him completely. His wholesome smile and evident interest in them have won him to them quickly."

William Wallace had been introduced to the Orient and they both liked what they saw.

3

Over the Language Barrier

Bill Wallace looked around the simple room in which he was to begin his individual language studies. Two chairs and a 24- by 36-inch table were the only furnishings.

On this first day, he was a little early, so he sat down and began glancing through some of the textbooks he had purchased. Thoroughly overwhelmed by the Chinese characters, he decided the script had been originated by a wild chicken in a print shop.

Just then the door opened and his language teacher, Mr. Wong, a highly correct Chinese scholar entered. Standing very erect, he stopped in front of Bill and smiled. Bill returned the smile and hastily stood to his feet. To his chagrin he towered a head and a half over his teacher. Mr. Wong looked him over slowly and in precise English with a British accent said, "They grow tall men where you come from."

The private language session began. Speaking in Chinese, Mr. Wong said, "Sit down," and reached gently up to Bill's shoulder to push him back into the chair from which he had just arisen. Then he smiled and said, again in Chinese, "Get up," and reached down and lifted him back to his feet. Action after action followed in the same pattern, and gradually Bill began to get the idea. Not a word of English was spoken in these classes; words and actions were matched and learned inductively. Though he felt stupid, clumsy, and even crude after an hour with Mr. Wong, Bill had to admit he already had learned something.

As the teacher pointedly pulled his watch from his pocket, Bill realized it was time for the class to be over. He returned to his room for an hour of private study. There he paced back and forth repeating the phrases he had heard from Mr. Wong and performing the indicated action to seal the association. Two hours later he went to another classroom which was just down the street from his boarding house to begin the more formal study.

This class was composed of an attractive group of new missionaries, including Mr. and Mrs. Eugene Hill, of Oklahoma, who were to become Bill's closest friends. Along with the Hills were Miss Auris Pender, of the Southern Baptist Mission, two Swedish-American missionaries, and a New Zealand Presbyterian.

In the first session they were introduced to Romanization, the process of taking Chinese sounds and reducing them to Romanized phonetics by substituting equivalent Roman letters for the Chinese characters. The teacher would write the statement, then Romanize it, then repeat it, and then have the class repeat it after him.

It was soon obvious that the astute Dr. Beddoe had rightly prophesied that his new colleague would have trouble learning Cantonese. The nonmusical surgeon was unable to reach many of the tones or, more frustrating, to recognize them. He often found himself furnishing comic relief for the class.

At the close of the morning sessions, the missionaries retired for lunch and more private study before they commenced their afternoon sessions, which again featured individual sessions followed by group recitation. They concluded at 4:30 in the afternoon, tried to get a bit of recreation or diversion, then gathered for dinner. After dinner, they retired to pore over the day's lessons, laboriously writing the Chinese characters and monotonously repeating the words and tones. They stopped only to wonder from time to time, with despair, if they would ever be able to master the language.

Bill was boarding in the spacious home of Mr. and Mrs. Harold Snuggs, veteran Southern Baptist missionaries to South China. At this time, Mr. Snuggs was treasurer of the South China Mission. Bill enjoyed living with the Snuggses; he enjoyed his friends, Eugene and Louise Hill; he enjoyed belonging to the mission group because it was almost like being a part of a family again—that was it, a big, happy family. The Snuggses met him at the boat when he returned from his visit to Wuchow and immediately took him to their hearts. Mrs. Snuggs, the motherly type, set herself up as the young surgeon's keeper.

Harold Snuggs reminded Bill of a college professor, and he began calling the older man "Professor." The term stuck, and within a couple of years most of the South China missionaries had adopted the name. Bill was deeply fond of the Snuggses and their young son, and undoubtedly the year he spent with them enabled him to make a much easier adjustment to his new life than might have been otherwise possible. He enjoyed it all, from his spacious room with the screened-in porch to the steady stream of visitors that came from the States—visitors for the centennial celebration of Baptist missions in China.

By this time single women missionaries all over China had heard of Bill's arrival, and it was remarkable how many of them found themselves in Canton from time to time. It became a subtle battle for the honor of sitting next to him at mission dinners, but he was not too discomfited by it. He became adept at being a charming, witty companion without betraying any awareness of the female wiles directed toward the downfall of his bachelorhood. This was his defense. It did not mean he was dedicated to bachelorhood— far from it—but he was dedicated to awaiting "the right girl."

Gene Hill and Bill, intrepid explorers, spent a great deal of time tramping about Canton together. Canton shopkeepers came to recognize the smiling twosome and enjoyed their efforts to practice the language on them. Being a bachelor, Bill had more time to himself, so he often struck out alone. He would rent a sampan and ride up and down the river that almost surrounds Canton, asking questions of his pilot and stopping from time to time at waterfront shops to converse with courteous storekeepers. Too, this proved to be a way to beat the Canton heat, and he often settled down with his books and notes on the front deck of a sampan for an afternoon of study.

Christmas brought letters and packages from home, and a bit of homesickness. A package from his sister contained a picture of his mother and father. Though the beautiful mother was only a faint memory and it had been three years since his beloved father had passed, Bill pictured himself again in the house on the corner of Broadway and Silver, listening to the happy sounds of the household. He could hear the melodious laugh of his mother and, with childlike pride, behold the quiet and efficient ministries of his physician-father. He could not but wonder if they understood the passion that now drove him, and the work to which he had committed his life.

His sister's missionary circle wanted to send him something and asked what he could really use. After some deliberation, he decided to make a rather large request. "You may subscribe to *Time* magazine for me, or to the bimonthly journal called *Surgical Clinics of North America.*"

Christmas also provided opportunity for a return trip to Wuchow. For two weeks he worked there almost day and night under a punishing surgical schedule. In a letter to his sister, he summed up the visit in three terse sentences. "I went to Wuchow and just got back yesterday. I had a good time. I operated."

Bill made many friends during his year of language school in Canton, and more than a few of them were among the Chinese. He had an innate way of relating to his adopted people that belied his background and training. In his natural modesty, he had a strange affinity with the Orientals that enabled him to communicate with them on a level that was not wholly verbal, but also intuitive—a level of feeling.

One of his close friends during this time was a young Christian teacher, Miss Roberta Ma, whose father was also a physician. She was a teacher at the Sun Yat-sen University and she introduced the inquisitive young doctor to the remarkable university and to the adjoining Memorial Park. They enjoyed walking along together discussing Chinese philosophy, sharing their common faith in Christ, and speculating about the future of the land which they both loved.

With her, Bill walked through the Temple of the Seven Hundred Genii at Kwan-Yin-Shan (Temple of the Goddess of Mercy) just to see what Buddhist temples look like. The young teacher interpreted intricacies of Chinese symbolism and mysteries of their ancient deities. Together they went window-shopping to practice Bill's dialect on the shopkeepers. She laughed at his horrible accent and was moved to tears by his dogged determination to learn the language.

And so, the year passed: hours of classroom recitation and determined study; delightful evenings with the Snuggses and fellow missionaries; exhausting games of tennis; long walks and bold explorations with Gene Hill; memorable moments with Chinese friends; high hours of needed spiritual refreshment and worship in the Canton Chinese churches.

Bill concluded his first year in China with a trip to Hong Kong to attend the annual South China Baptist Mission meeting which was held in August, 1936. Following the mission meeting, Bill started for Wuchow.

War was brewing between the belligerent warlords of Kwangsi Province, in which Wuchow was located, and the Nationalist Government headed by Chiang Kai-shek. The Generalissimo had given Kwangsi a deadline to come to terms, after which he would attack. The Kwangsi warlords responded by fortifying the city of Wuchow and moving troops and guns to the border just below Wuchow. Chiang then brought his crack troops, fresh from battles with the Communists in the west, to a staging area near Canton. The West River steamer would have to run this gauntlet to reach Wuchow.

Fortunately, the West River steamer was not going into the hornet's nest unprotected. Three gunboats, two British and one American, were sent into Kwangsi to protect the interest of their countrymen in that area. They accompanied the West River steamer into Wuchow, and except for a few wild shots and some yelling from the riverbank, they made the trip without incident.

4

Waa I Saang

Upon reaching Wuchow, Bill Wallace found he was the only missionary there. The others had decided to wait out the crisis in Hong Kong. Outwardly undisturbed, Bill went right to the hospital, deposited his belongings, and the next day was in surgery. That afternoon he received an American naval officer who had come from the gunboat, the USS *Mindanao,* which had anchored in the West River off Wuchow. The captain sent his compliments and offered to take Bill on board and give him safe transportation back to Hong Kong.

"Back to Hong Kong!" exclaimed Bill. "Why, I just got here and I'm not going anywhere, war or no war."

"Begging your pardon, sir," the young officer replied. "The captain feels that he cannot be responsible for your safety if you remain in the city even overnight."

Bill laughed. "Tell your captain to rest easy. He was not responsible for my coming here in the first place, and he doesn't need to be responsible for my staying here." Then, more seriously, "But tell him I do appreciate his concern. I know he wanted to help; I just don't think I need it."

Bill watched the sailor depart and then turned back to his Chinese resident and said, "All right now, let's look at that O.B. case. Did you say it was a breech presentation?"

By evening the naval officer was back again. When Bill came down from surgery and saw him, the American was grinning rather sheepishly. "Excuse me for interrupting you again, Dr. Wallace, but the captain would like to know if you would at least come aboard this evening for dinner."

"Your captain would not be trying to trick me into safety, now, would he?"

"Oh, no, sir. It is the captain's birthday and he wanted another American to share it with him."

"Well, in that case, tell the captain I'll be delighted. I'm still having trouble with chopsticks anyway."

It was a strange birthday party held on the USS *Mindanao* in the middle of the West River that September evening. Other than Bill, two oil company men planning to spend the next couple of days on board were also present. They had a good time. After ascertaining where the others were from and something of their background and discovering the one or two acquaintances in common, the captain asked Bill the inevitable question: "Why would an able young surgeon like you give his life to a 'God-forsaken place' like this?"

Bill smiled. He had heard that question before, and he was sure he would hear it again. "It's not an easy thing to explain," he said. "I am not running away from anything. I have not had any disappointing love affairs, and, so far as I know, the police blotter's never borne my name."

They laughed at his obvious good humor, but the captain pressed the point. "But what makes a man feel he should do something like this?"

Bill said, "Well, my father was a doctor, but that was the last thing I wanted to be. My love was mechanics. A gasoline motor or even an electrical motor is still one of the most intriguing things in the world to me. But as a teen-ager I came to experience a deep sense of unrest about what I was to do with my life. One day, I became very deeply convinced that I should become a medical missionary."

"Had you ever considered anything like that before?" One of the oil men posed the question.

"No, I am certain no one had ever suggested it. My father was all set to help me get into the automobile business, but after that day, I was convinced that this was what I should do."

Bill paused, caught up in his own memories, and then went on. "That was eleven years ago now, and I have become more and more sure with each passing year that God was in this decision."

Getting up and walking to the porthole, he said, "I am convinced that happiness, fulfilment, and meaning for me lie right up there on that hill."

There was a long silence and Bill became a little embarrassed. "But I don't want to sound pious or mystic or heroic. Actually, I am the world's worst preacher; I am a proven coward; and I am only a tolerable surgeon."

At this, his companions smiled and soon the conversation went in other directions. But his witness had been borne, and these men would not soon forget the smiling young Tennessean with whom they celebrated a birthday party in the middle of the West River while waiting for a war.

The war turned out to be one of few bullets and many words. Two weeks later all was settled; the other missionaries returned, and things began to assume a normal appearance around the Stout Memorial Hospital.

Within a week after the war threat had subsided, the annual flooding of the West River came, bringing more devastation than the war possibly could have. The Kwangsi troops had sent heavily loaded barges into the narrow gorges below Wuchow, hoping to dam up the river there and confound the Generalissimo's efforts. When the war was settled, they were not able to remove the barges before the West River and the Fu River began to disgorge the tons of water that had been deposited in the hills and mountains by the September rains. In a matter of hours, the water backed up until a third of the city was inundated and a strong current was flowing down the main street. As if by magic, thousands of sampans appeared in the streets carrying people to and fro. They had been through this before, but Bill Wallace was beginning to wonder if things ever became normal in China.

True to his word, Dr. Beddoe engaged a language teacher for Bill so he could begin his second year of study. His afternoons were given completely to language study, and under no circumstances was he ever to be interrupted. Somehow, incredibly, this schedule was kept throughout the year. However, Bill operated every morning and was on the hospital floors much of the night trying to stanch just a bit of the flow of suffering and disease that came through the Stout Memorial Hospital.

Long before daylight, he would report to the hospital to study his cases, supervise prepping, and instruct his assistants. Before breakfast, he had usually completed an operation, or, if they were minor, several of them. The range of work he was called on to do was unbelievable.

Bill was soon thanking God for the two years of surgery he had as a resident at Knoxville General and wishing fervently that he had had three more. In a few weeks he performed operations he never expected to be called upon to do and met situations for which he did not know there was a precedent. He did more goiter operations than he had thought possible. He removed tumors of incredible size, performed delicate eye operations, and harelip and cleft palate surgery was almost commonplace. Appendectomies, amputations, complicated obstetric cases—the list was endless. He began to acquire a reputation.

Bill performed a successful operation on a little girl with a bad harelip. The child could talk clearly and the mother, grateful that her little girl was no longer laughed at by her playmates, nor taunted with rocks and sticks, went to see every sick person that she knew and told them about the wonderful Waa I Saang in Wuchow.

One day she heard of a woman who was distressed over her clubfooted boy. The husband had threatened to throw the child away. The grateful mother took her little girl and went to see the woman.

"Go to see Waa I Saang in Wuchow!" the grateful mother exclaimed. "See what he did to my child. She can talk clearly now and looks like other children, too. Waa I Saang can do anything. Why, he can give your child a new foot."

The incident gave Bill a deep sense of satisfaction. Not that someone should think he could do miracles, but that a child no longer had to be the butt of persecution and cruel jesting. For these opportunities to rejoice, however—and there were countless numbers of them—there was a balancing factor, a never-too-long-absent sense of failure and frustration that came when the battle was lost and a life slipped away.

A small child had been admitted with advanced diphtheria. Bill employed every possible kind of emergency treatment, but despite all of his efforts, including a tracheotomy, the child died. Slowly he straightened his shoulders and sighed. Then he reached down and picked up the lifeless child, and, gently holding it in his arms, he sat down on the bed, looking into the closed eyes and still face. As the parents were brought in, he told them in his halting Cantonese, but with a tenderness that broke through any linguistic limitations, exactly what had happened. Then he told them of the Christ and how he loved the little children.

The hospital occupancy grew steadily and its reputation spread as never before. Dr. Robert E. Beddoe was jubilant over the turn of events. That fall he wrote Dr. Maddry:

"Dr. Wallace has already demonstrated that the Board made no mistake in selecting him for this place. He has a keen eye, a steady hand, and a good knowledge of surgical techniques. When he finally can give his total time to the hospital, I have every confidence that he will build up a reputation that will bring patients here even from Canton."

Later, Dr. Beddoe reported a 50 per cent increase in number of patients in the months since Bill had come to the hospital's ministry. He also reported a revival at the hospital. "Best of all are the spiritual results. We are swept from joy to joy as people of all classes are saved. There have been two cases of entire families being saved. . . . Dr. Leung joined our church recently and our fine lady doctor, Miss Wang, is to be baptized Sunday. Truly God has richly blessed us this year."

These two doctors, planting their lives with Christ against the traditions of their land and all the pressures that their heritage brought against them, reflected the power of the witness of the one who had come into their midst. The Chinese had heard sermons before, but in Bill Wallace they began to see one, and that made the difference.

Bill was indescribably happy. He was needed, he was seeing

people healed, he was where he felt God wanted him. "My cup runneth over."

Bill's second Christmas in China passed with less nostalgia than the first one. A little bit of Tennessee arrived with a big box of homemade fruit cake, the gift of Ruth Lynn and her husband, Sydney. Then the small gifts exchanged with the mission staff and a brief visit to Hong Kong helped a growing sense of belonging.

The situation in China seemed more stable. Only a brief, isolated political incident marred the scene following the settlement of the Kwangsi war.

Chiang Kai-shek went into one of his northern provinces to confer with a warlord. While he was there, the Communists made a bold, daylight attack, overpowered his small entourage, and kidnapped the Generalissimo. They demanded he grant them new powers and administrative controls within the central government. Infuriated, the Chinese leader demanded instead that he be put to death. Many of the Communists were in favor of doing this, but, instead, Chiang was released that a common front could be established against Japan. The Generalissimo had little choice and an alliance was effected which brought a temporary peace and a semblance of unity to China. Ostensibly, they turned together to meet the more immediate threat of China's mortal enemy—Japan.

For five years the Japanese had been planning the conquest of China. After taking Manchuria, they had systematically begun seizing chunks of Chinese territory north of the Great Wall. This was done while the Chinese were embroiled in internal disputes. After Chiang Kai-shek's kidnapping and the tentative alliance reached with the Communists, however, Japan realized she was faced with the prospects of a united China which could totally change a situation that had been going her way. If she were going to take China, she had to move now.

Thus, on the night of July 7, 1937, Japanese garrison troops were engaged in field maneuvers just across the river from Peking. At the Marco Polo Bridge, someone fired a shot. The Japanese quickly claimed that they had been assaulted and launched a massive "retaliation." War had begun.

The days and weeks that followed horrified and shocked the world which, for all the somber warnings in Europe and Asia, could not yet believe that which, to many astute observers, was inevitable. The Japanese crushed the Chinese with ruthless efficiency wherever they met them. The rape of Nanking, the senseless slaughter of millions, the wanton destruction soon became history.

Bill Wallace and the missionaries at the Stout Memorial Hospital were following these events closely. In the first place, the North China Mission was immediately involved, and the stories that came back were not pretty. Many of the missionaries elected to stay through the Japanese assault to carry on their work, as best they could, behind the lines. Secondly, even an armchair strategist knew that the West River Basin from Canton to Nanning would certainly be one of the premium targets in Japanese war plans. Wuchow was right in the middle.

Thousands of Kwangsi troops were shipped to Canton and then north, and soon the reports began to come back of their slaughter. A great wail arose from the people of Wuchow. Then Canton and the railroad were bombed, and finally the river itself was blockaded.

Now the doctors were faced by shortage of both food and medical supplies. Fortunately for the hospital, Dr. Beddoe was a very able and wise administrator, and with precise planning and almost uncanny foresight he stayed ahead of each new crisis, always seeming to be able to lay his hands on needed supplies. Invariably, he had stored strategic items in quantities that sufficed when there were long periods in which they could get none.

Dr. Beddoe's concern went beyond the Stout Memorial Hospital at this time, however, for the Baptist hospital at Kweilin—a Baptist mission station farther west and north in the Kwangsi Province—was without administrative leadership. Soon it would have no alternative but to close. Dr. Beddoe wanted desperately to go over there and save the institution. His decision not to go brought to the surface some feelings concerning his new colleague. He wrote the Board:

"At this moment I believe for me to turn completely loose of the Stout Memorial Hospital would seriously endanger its prosperity. I have no exalted opinions of my importance or abilities, but I do know that Wallace is not ready yet to assume responsibility of this great and rapidly growing institution. . . . I have observed him closely and must say that he is not ready to take charge of the Stout Memorial Hospital. Aside from the fact that he greatly dislikes administrative work, is the fact that he does not yet have a grasp of the Chinese nature and psychology which is far more important than a knowledge of the language."

Several things contributed to this attitude. Bill seemed interested only in the medical side of his work and actually spurned any administrative responsibility or detail. He referred everything that came his way of this nature to Dr. Beddoe and left all decisions up to the administrator, even when he was consulted. Also, Bill seemed to be a soft touch for the Chinese and his reticence in charging was already widely known. As a disciplinarian, he let both nurses and doctors choose their own pace; he was never heard to reprimand. Dr. Beddoe saw this as a complete absence of administrative faculty, a dearth of understanding of the Chinese mind, and a lack of appreciation for the fiscal responsibilities of the hospital.

But there was another side to this picture. Bill scrupulously wanted to avoid any sign of seeming to aspire to the administrator's job or to getting over into the realm of his responsibility. Too, he relished the opportunity to concentrate on his medicine, to have the details handled by the able Beddoe. While his leadership of the hospital staff did not give the outward appearance of being dynamic, the fact was that they did follow him enthusiastically and even sacrificially. He did have a certain amount of naïvete concerning the Chinese nature and psychology, but even in these early years, it was balanced by his intuitive empathy with them.

In late October, Dr. Beddoe no longer had time to consider the Kweilin situation or even Bill Wallace's administrative shortcomings. The American consul had warned the hospital staff to prepare to evacuate, and the mission group were forced to talk about what they would do in case the order came. As yet, Japanese planes had not appeared over Wuchow skies, but the missionaries realized that there was a strong possibility that they would, and bring destruction they winced to think about. The staff, and especially the missionaries, found they had emotional ties to the old hospital that they had not before suspected.

The hospital had an unbroken ministry since 1904, and the missionaries were all the more anxious that it not be interrupted— even at the threat of Japanese occupation. Thus, at the conclusion of their first meeting on the subject, they wrote Dr. Maddry: "We at the hospital have decided to stay under all conditions. We feel that now is the time when every hospital in China should be open."

On the 19th of December, Bill Wallace opened his eyes and lay still until he grew accustomed to the darkness, punctuated only by a faint shaft of light emanating from the hospital across the garden. Quietly he slipped out of bed—he lived in the Beddoe household since coming to Wuchow and did not want to wake the others—dressed and slipped out into the predawn mist that was rolling up from the river below. Within moments he was visiting wards, checking patients, and reading the night nurse's reports. After checking out some patients and giving instructions to be called at a certain time, he returned to his small cubicle of an office to study X-rays that were to guide his surgery for the day. He made notes in a broad, almost unintelligible hand, then yawned and stretched—the movement of a man content with his lot—savoring the beginning of another day.

Thumbing the pages of his New Testament—the same one in which he had so long ago marked his determination to be a medical missionary--he began his morning devotions. He read a brief passage of Scripture, gave some thought to it, made a few mental notes, and bowed his head for a brief prayer. In a few moments—he was not known for long devotions—he arose and walked out on the porch of the hospital to greet the dawn.

There was something fascinating about the way dawn came at

Wuchow. It seemed to have to do with the river and the mist and
the boats and the nets; it was somehow related to the green banyan
tree that dominated the hospital compound and the greener bamboo
that lined the shore of the Fu to his right; it was tied in with the
good, clean feeling of a new start. Bill always enjoyed it. Smiling,
thoroughly happy, he took the steps three at a time and jogged
toward the Beddoe house to have breakfast with Dr. and Mrs.
Beddoe and Rex Ray.

"Howdy, Bill." It was the traditional greeting of the genial
Texan, Rex Ray. "I was just explaining to Dr. Beddoe my plan for
running the Japanese blockade next spring in order to get medical
supplies you 'sawbones' are going to need."

"I am afraid our intrepid cowboy-adventurer is anxious to relive
the old days," dryly remarked Dr. Beddoe. It was well-known that
Rex Ray had been captured by a Chinese bandit a decade before
and he never tired of telling of the exciting adventure. "But I
hardly think the plan is wise, despite the fact we will have some
very critical needs by spring."

"What's your plan, Parson?" Bill liked to talk with the indomitable old missionary, whom he had nicknamed.

Enthusiastically, Ray began to outline his plan. "You see, I
have this friend who owns a junk in Canton. . . ."

Dr. Beddoe interrupted him. "If you ask me, Canton won't be
in Chinese hands by spring. They bombed it again this morning,
and eighteen Japanese warships are reported on their way to begin
a bombardment."

"That doesn't sound good," Bill said. He had meant to get back
in time that morning to listen to the news with Dr. Beddoe, a kind
of morning ritual for the two, but surgical preparation had prevented his doing so.

Suddenly an air-raid siren fractured the morning peace. The
three men had heard it before in practice drills, but this was the
real thing; they could hear for themselves the distant roar of
planes. They ran down the steps from the house and across to the
hospital. Near panic prevailed, but working calmly, they organized
the excited staff and quieted the terrified patients. Then, beginning

with the top floor, they moved the more serious patients to the basement. By this time they could hear bombs exploding and the terrifying chatter of machine guns. The ambulatory patients walked down the steps, helping those who could not. If the bombs hit the hospital, they would have to go through five floors of concrete. While the builders could not have foreseen the need, they had built an excellent bomb shelter.

As soon as the patients were safely in the basement, Bill bounded up the five flights of stairs to the roof to watch the sky. There were eleven planes in flight. A big red-rising-sun emblem sparkled from the nearest.

The first bombs fell nearly a mile away, at Wuchow's airport, completely demolishing the hangar where the Chinese planes were based. Then the marauders made a run at the electrical plant, and failing to destroy it, they circled for a second pass. Again they missed, but this time the bombs fell nearer the hospital and the explosion shook the building, shattering glass.

It was over as quickly as it began, and as the planes disappeared over the hill back of the hospital, the all-clear sounded. Bill looked over the city. Fires were blazing away in more than a dozen places and a shroud of smoke was beginning to gather overhead like a ghostly umbrella. People were running to and fro, and chaos was king. Bill Wallace later explained that he would never be the same again, that attacks might get worse, much worse, but there was nothing like the first time!

5

Trial by Fire

"I think we ought to go ahead and talk about it now." Dr. Beddoe was speaking in an intent, studied manner. The Wuchow missionaries were gathered for an informal meeting in the Beddoes' living room.

"It may seem remote now, but events point to an eventual Japanese campaign against South China. If Canton falls, they may move right up the river to Wuchow. Or it would be comparatively easy for their troops to march against us from Watlum after blockading the West River with naval units."

Rex-Ray spoke. "You can bet your bottom dollar, if they start in here to take us, they will try to level us to the ground with their bombers first. I am not sure there would be enough of us left to worry about when they got here."

"I don't agree," said Beddoe. "Sporadic or even continuous air raids will not close this hospital or stampede this staff. We can take a direct hit or even several hits on our roof and still stand. I know this building; I built it."

"Well, they may be unable to level the building," Bill said. Standing at the window, he was looking up at the gray stone structure. "I agree with you there. But it's kind of difficult to carry on much of a hospital if all the equipment, windows, and doors are shattered. Maybe we ought to set up emergency operating facilities in the basement where concussion is least likely to do serious damage." He had given this matter a lot of thought and was glad for the opportunity to introduce the idea.

"I think Bill's right," Mrs. Beddoe said. "It won't be too difficult to set it up if we start now."

Dr. Beddoe nodded. "I agree; but the thing I'm trying to point out is that military occupation is another matter altogether. Since learning of the behavior of Japanese troops at Nanking, I have been trying to formulate a plan of action in the event Wuchow falls. I am unwilling to ask these nurses to remain at their posts and run the risk of violation by drunken soldiers."

At this statement they were all silent. The stories coming from Nanking were revolting.

Surprisingly, Bill, who seldom offered advice, spoke again. "Let's take measures against air raids now and concern ourselves with invasion when it comes. I doubt that we can make much advance preparation in that direction anyhow."

A murmur of approval came from the others. It was not a note of resignation or fatalism, but one of "Let's work while it's day; we know the night is coming." Bill believed strongly in the Scripture passage which, in effect, says, "As your days are, so shall your strength be."

Two months later the bombers returned. This time it was a much larger flight of planes, and following the bomb run, they turned and came in low, mercilessly machine-gunning all who were unfortunate enough to be exposed.

Though the missionaries had completed preparation on the emergency operating room, the attack caught Bill in regular surgery. He barely had time to complete his suturing and secure his patient in a hallway away from flying glass when the first bombs fell. Again the hospital was spared, though much glass was broken by concussion. The number of wounded brought in following the raid was twice that of the first raid.

Efforts to repair the carnage wrought by the planes continued far into the night. Bill was doing a totally different kind of surgery now—trying to put together violently rent flesh, tying off stumps of limbs, seeking to restore some semblance of form to mangled features. If he loved to see surgery as a place for artistic re-creation, he now faced it as a man standing in the middle of a broken dike, trying desperately to stem a raging current with a few pitiful and futile sandbags.

Weeks later, tired and exasperated, Bill said to a Chinese colleague, "I sometimes feel like I am plowing in the sea."

"You should take a vacation," his colleague replied.

Missionaries under Bill's Board were supposed to take a month a year for rest and renewal, but Bill had taken only one week in three years. With the Japanese overrunning much of China, he decided he had better see some of the country now if he ever meant to. He would visit the interior of China, where Western culture had made its least impact. He would immerse himself in Chinese life for a time. After all, Beddoe was always saying he did not understand the Chinese mind and psychology, though in rare moments Bill wondered if he did not understand it better than Beddoe. At any rate, Bill decided it would give him some time to work through this depression of frustration that was settling over him.

Dr. Beddoe had strong reservations about the venture. Bill hoped to go west to Chungking and Chengtu, and in doing so he would leave Cantonese-speaking territory. He would be unable to communicate. Bill said that he still could read it and he always could contact missionaries in the area. Seeing that his colleague had his mind made up, Beddoe relented.

The last week in March, Bill performed an incredible number of surgical procedures in order to leave without any known need unmet. Then, exhausted, he left by bus on the first day of April.

His first day of travel was over the low mountains northwest of Wuchow to Watlum. The bus, crowded and hot, featured a babble of voices and an unsortable array of smells. Despite the discomfort, Bill found himself relaxing and enjoying the countryside with its dazzling green blanket of new rice shoots. By noon he had struck up conversations with the people jammed closest to him, surprising them with his Chinese—horrible accent and all.

Watlum is an old, walled city. Nearly all of China's cities were originally little fortresses defended by local warlords, but New China had seen the destruction of many of these walls under the impact of expansion. Watlum was an exception. Its wall sheltered a city of Old China with charm that was a Western visitor's delight, and inconvenience that was his bane. It was as yet untouched by Japanese bombs.

Before this trip, much of what Bill had experienced was thoroughly westernized. However, being totally immersed in Chinese life as he had wished, exceeded anything he had bargained for. Before the first day was over, he remembered it was April Fool's Day and decided the joke was on him.

The pinch on food was only beginning to be felt in the western provinces. The traveler with money had no problem in letting his appetite explore all that he felt was palatable: crispy yellowfish, crackling with hot sweet-and-pungent sauce, melons steamed to perfection with bits of ham, cabbage, and chicken within its wells, chicken velvet, bamboo shoots, pigeon eggs, Peking duck with tiny dough blankets, lotus and orange soup, luscious wine mushrooms. Bill tried them all, but his Spartan-like habits soon confined most of his experimentation to rice in its various forms.

Two days out of Wuchow, he entered Mandarin-speaking country and lost the freedom of communication he enjoyed in Cantonese after his two years of study. But he could read Mandarin and get along fairly well. He delighted in people and sights and sounds and smells. What would seem for many to be a lonely vacation, turned into an exotic journey for the young doctor.

As he began to recuperate from the exhausting routine he had followed the past year, he was able to drink deeply of the traditional and colorful life of these people to whom he had given himself.

From Luichow he continued cross-country by rail into terrain dominated by the great Yangtze River system. Bill's immediate destination in Szechwan was the ancient city of Chungking. By the time he arrived, he was aware of how little he had learned about life in China in his three years. Because his skills had been so vitally needed, he had been spared little time to become acquainted with this ageless world.

Chungking, a walled city of some 200,000 in the spring of 1938 when Bill saw it, was steeped in Chinese history. Its people were usually the last in China to embrace any new dynasty, and the least enthusiastic in supporting whoever was in power. However, it was among these very people that Sun Yat-sen initiated his successful 1911 revolution against the Manchus. Within months it was to become the provisional capital of Nationalist China.

At this time, Chungking and the Szechwan Province were controlled by a network of semifeudal alliances under a warlord. It had grown up to service the peasant economy of western China. They brought their silk and meat and rice and exchanged them for kerosene and cloth and thread. Its wall encircled the peninsula on which it was located, and it encompassed nine great gates through which its traffic was channeled. Eight of the gates opened onto the cliffs overlooking the Yangtze. A ninth, called the Gate Connecting with Distant Place, was the old imperial road that led through the valleys to Chengtu.

After securing one of the few rooms available (already the city was beginning to be overrun by the refugees from the northeast), Bill went to one of the flourishing mission hospitals there and made contact with another missionary doctor. Though they had never met before, they became fast friends, and, exchanging insights and problems from their respective work, they spent a few enjoyable days together.

Bill was introduced to the city from an insider's point of view. He saw the open sores of opium traffic, cholera, dysentery, syphilis, and the ravages of trachoma. The doctor showed him some of the competition for his healing art: the herb doctors who mysteriously mixed weird recipes calling for everything from children's urine to musk crystals. And a live rooster bound to the chest of a corpse would do wonders in keeping away evil spirits.

As they walked down the old streets, dodging squealing pigs, squawking hens, and heavily laden coolies singing their age-old chants, Bill asked his friend the question that he was struggling with in his own ministry. "How do you ever get used to the idea that you are going to be able to make such a small impression upon all this suffering—even in a lifetime?"

His friend smiled. "You're tackling a problem that almost did me in, my first term of service. I believe every missionary faces it. A kind of crisis of compassion. You can either narrow your eyes against it and harden your heart—and all of us do that to a degree—or you can let it drive you to a frenzy that will break you. Those are the extreme reactions, of course. I finally had to face the fact that God is fully aware of my limitations, and he brought me here for a purpose. I must do what my hand finds to do to the best of my ability. But, I must leave the statistics up to God, even as I have to leave the course of history up to him."

Bill said gloomily, "I am more aware of my limitations than I have ever been. I guess my problem is that I have been imposing my limitations on God."

"Each of us has to make this adjustment by himself. Some never do. It's a time when a missionary's faith is tried to its foundation and his emotional strength is tested to its core."

Bill pondered his friend's words for a long time.

He saw Chungking just before it became a new city. Six months later it became the hub of Free China and swelled to four times its original size.

From Chungking, Bill went to Chengtu, a great university center, soon to be the center of most of the great universities of China. Here he saw east and west in contrast. Women dressed in the latest Western fashions walked beside others in traditional Chinese fashions, who hobbled down the street with their tiny, deformed feet, bound since childhood as a beauty mark.

Bill spent nearly a week here visiting the universities and the hospitals. He conferred with missionaries in the area and studied new techniques in surgery. Actually, methods developed at this time in China by sheer necessity were unique and untried elsewhere in the world.

Despite his reticence, Bill Wallace had a remarkable facility for meeting people and learning from them. People would be amazed after having spent some time with him as to how much they had talked and how little he had talked and how little they had noticed that.

After a week, Bill bade his new friends at Chengtu farewell and boarded a colorful river steamer for a voyage down the mighty Yangtze River to Hankow. The Japanese had already mounted their spring campaign and had just taken Suchow. Their next objective was Hankow, but at the time Bill booked his passage, the floods from the Yellow River had slowed their offensive and he decided to see this remarkably industrialized city while he had the chance. It took him two more weeks to get from Hankow through the Hunan Province back into Kwangsi.

Totally caught up in his odyssey, Bill had neglected to keep in touch with the people at Wuchow. As a result, Dr. Beddoe was deeply worried when, after five weeks, no word had come. He had written Dr. Maddry earlier that he had felt that it was unwise for Bill to go, but pointed out that there was no deterring him. Bill Wallace's pleasant obstinancy was often a source of exasperation to the dedicated administrator.

The two men still did not understand each other, though they had a deep mutual respect. Bill's tendency to be very reticent and uncommunicative around highly authoritative persons, only aggravated the problem. But one of the remarkable facts of his life was the gradual winning of Dr. Beddoe. Through the years, the administrator saw his young colleague develop and demonstrate to a remarkable degree some of the very characteristics he felt the young man so lacked.

In the middle of May, Bill Wallace arrived in Wuchow refreshed and enthusiastic. He was more at peace than at any time since coming to China.

The city was bombed for the third time in two weeks after Bill returned. A week later the plane that flew between Hong Kong and Chungking, making a regular stop at Wuchow, was shot down just south of the city and its escaping passengers were machine-gunned to their death. Up to this time, the staff of Stout Memorial Hospital felt that the Japanese would not intentionally bomb them. On the roof they painted a gigantic American flag and on either side of it huge crosses.

All feeling of security disappeared on September 17, 1938. The siren sounded its eerie warning at midmorning as Bill Wallace was involved in an intricate, extremely dangerous abdominal operation. As the piercing wail reached the operating team, they froze for an instant, then, as one, turned to look questioningly at the surgeon.

His voice was muffled by his mask, but its tone was calm and authoritative. "Miss Luk, Dr. Leung, stay with me. The rest of you help the staff get the patients to the basement; then go there yourselves."

"But Waa I Saang, the Japanese?"

"Do what I say. We are not finished here and we certainly cannot stop."

Beads of perspiration glistened on his normally dry forehead. Miss Luk sponged his head; the operation went on.

They were almost finished when they heard the planes, first a drone, then, like the string section in a symphony of horror, they heard the high whine of the dive bombers. Unconsciously, Bill spread his feet, bracing himself against the expected concussion. He was closing the incision, suturing with remarkable speed and dexterity. Again, he looked up. "You go now; they will need you."

"But, Doctor, what about you and the patient?"

"I will move him into the ward at the end of the hall where the windows have not been replaced. It will be less dangerous." His last words were all but lost as explosions came—some dull, thudding, as if at a great distance; others earsplitting, frighteningly close. "Go! Hurry!" It was a command.

Outside, terror reigned over the chaotic scene. In back alleys and along tiny streets dozens of men, women, and children were roasted to death by raging fires. Up wide thoroughfares red tracer bullets danced a jig of death, leaving behind twisted remnants of life. In the few shelters the living huddled on top of those crushed to death in the panic. Inside the hospital courtyard, hundreds of Chinese crouched, hoping that the American flag and the red crosses on top of the great building would provide safety.

Shortly after the first bombs fell, Bill Wallace completed his surgery and rolled his patient into the big ward on the top floor, as he had said he would do. His choice was simple. The patient could not be moved downstairs and there was some protection here from concussion because all the glass had been broken. As the patient came back to consciousness, Bill leaned over him to hold him on the bed, trying all the time to reassure him in his Tennessee-accented Cantonese.

Then a segment of the Japanese attacking force turned on the hospital compound. Nineteen bombs exploded within the supposedly neutral area dedicated to mercy. The building shook as if it would disintegrate.

One of the bombs landed on the roof immediately over the place where Bill hovered with his patient. The explosion sent plaster and debris everywhere and left a gaping hole in the roof; chair, bed, doctor, and patient were flung across the floor. In the remarkable providence of a merciful God, neither doctor nor patient was injured. With that final act, the planes departed and the city was left to its grief.

As soon as the planes left, the staff members rushed from the basement to the top floor where they found Bill and the patient praying together—a halting, poorly phrased, but thoroughly sincere prayer. When the staff saw Bill and his patient safe, they fell on them with cries of joy and knelt to give their own prayers of thanksgiving.

It was an act of bravery which would have won the Medal of Honor for a soldier on the battlefield. God does not have ceremonies in this life for his heroes, but the Scriptures speak of a time in the eternity to come when the heavens will take note. The legend of Bill Wallace was taking shape.

The wounded began to pour in. They were coming up the hill, some carried on broken doors, charred boards, and even in baskets. For Bill Wallace and his staff it was the beginning of a nightmare that refused to end. They cut, clamped, and stitched some semblance of humanity back into the torn and mutilated. They groaned with frustration when life eluded their frantic fingers and rejoiced when victory seemed to be theirs.

The waiting room looked like a slaughter house: the broken, bruised, torn, and bleeding bodies of men, women, and children were everywhere. Every bed in the hospital held a victim. And up and down the corridors lay suffering people of all ages and all sizes, helpless, groaning, and dying. Bill asked Ray to take charge of the waiting room and help the doctors and nurses bring in only the most seriously wounded. Ray reached down to pick a little girl from the cold concrete. A shrapnel piece had torn her innocent little face, and as the missionary picked her up, the last color faded from her cheeks and seemed to disappear in a little red rivulet that wound its way across the floor.

Later, the exhausted, hollow-eyed doctor stood in his red-stained white operating coat, looking over the city of Wuchow. A third of it had been destroyed and thousands of people were homeless and hungry—or dead. He remembered his Chungking friend's advice. "You do what you are able to do and you leave the statistics to the Lord."

The next morning the missionaries set up a soup kitchen in front of the clinic and served rice soup with a few sparse vegetables.

A cable to the American consul told of the bombing and a strong diplomatic protest was relayed to Tokyo. It did little good.

Dr. Bill Wallace's trial term was becoming a trial by fire.

6

Incident in Canton

Eugene Hill stood on the Canton dock watching the passengers debark from the West River steamer. In a moment he spotted the man he was meeting. Tall and smiling, dressed in a tropical white suit, Bill Wallace sprang to the dock and warmly greeted his friend. Gene noted that his youthful appearance and lighthearted greeting belied the experience of the past few months —except for his eyes. They were more mature, the eyes of a young veteran. There was a new toughness of spirit in him like a tempered blade.

"Well, Doctor, I expected you to stay up there in your nice, safe Kwangsi retreat. There's a war down here, you know."

"I was dying from boredom and I had to have some excitement," sighed the young Tennessean, delighted to have an opportunity to respond to Gene Hill's droll wit again.

Gene laughed. "Seriously, when the Japanese landed at Bias Bay last week, I thought surely Dr. Beddoe would forbid you to come to the executive meeting."

"Well," Bill admitted with a grin, "he wasn't exactly enthusiastic about my coming."

Gene replied, "He knows what a stubborn surgeon he has, and he has probably resigned himself to it with good Christian grace." He laughed and gave Bill a friendly slap on the back.

"Why, the executive committee business is a rather important honor," Bill said. "I'm not going to let the Japanese do me out of it."

"What do you mean, 'honor'? They elected us to the committee because they knew we were foolish enough to come to a meeting like this, bombings and all."

Laughing together, they climbed into rickshas for the ride to

46

Hill's home where Bill would stay. As they rode along, Gene explained the situation.

"Bill, I came within an inch of telegraphing you today to tell you not to come. We thought we would have plenty of time to meet and conclude our business in time for you to get back home, but I am not so sure now. The Japanese have not fallen into the Generalissimo's plans at all. He set up strong fortifications along the Pearl River, but the Japanese landed at Bias Bay and their tanks are moving across the rice fields which, due to the drought, are rock-hard. They are meeting only token resistance. Unless the Chinese can regroup forces within the next day or two, nothing can stop them from rolling in here by the latter part of this week."

Bill gave a soft whistle. "I didn't realize they could get here that fast. I figured that, even if the invasion group proved larger than we heard, delaying action could keep them out for at least another ten days." He paused and then asked, "What about Louise? Isn't she expecting pretty soon?"

Gene was serious. "Yes, she is. I tried to get her to go out to Hong Kong, but she is even more stubborn than a certain doctor I know."

"She's just afraid to leave you," Bill kidded. "She knows you wouldn't know what to do without her."

"Man, that's closer to the truth than you realize!" exclaimed Gene. "But I do have a plan. I have rented an apartment on Sha-Mein and Dr. Hayes has agreed to look after her. She should be safe there."

Bill nodded in agreement. Sha-Mein was a foreign concession area separated from Canton proper by a narrow canal about fifty feet wide. So far, the Japanese had not violated its neutrality. They had honored concessions elsewhere, and the missionaries thought they probably would here.

"That's a good idea, Gene. I think she will be better off there," Bill agreed. "But what are you going to do about the seminary?"

Gene was professor at Graves Theological Seminary, which stood on a hill at the edge of Canton.

"We are dismissing classes Wednesday, and the Chinese faculty and students are leaving immediately," Gene said. "If the Chinese resist right into the city, that seminary is not going to be a very safe place. The hospital is closing, too, and the patients have been either dismissed or sent up the river. Most of the medical staff will go up country or to Hong Kong."

Bill said, "I am surprised to see so many people and cars still in the streets. I would have thought the bombings would bring this place to a standstill."

"It gets quiet quickly," said Gene. "A small flight came over early this morning. You can see some smoke over to the left at this next corner. That's where most of the bombs hit. They are government buildings."

"Well, one thing is certain," Bill said grimly: "this will be one of the shortest executive committee meetings in the history of the South China Mission."

"It will be if I have anything to do with it," said Gene.

And it was. By the second afternoon all the emergency decisions before the executive committee had been cleared, and letters, telegrams, and cablegrams were dispatched accordingly. Just before the meeting adjourned, a large flight of Japanese bombers hit Canton. The committee's meeting place in Dr. Hayes' office on Sha-Mein was not hit, but the explosions around them and the staccato of machine gun bullets were disconcerting.

Now the problem for the upcountry members of the committee was to get out. Alec Herring, one of the executive committee members, secured transportation on a Standard Oil launch to Hong Kong. Bill decided to wait until early the next morning to try to get a boat.

The next morning, Bill worked his way through the masses of people jamming streets that led to the main bridge out of Canton. He finally reached the docks. He might as well have been trying to go to the moon. Not even a sampan was available. The regular boats had canceled, and foreign gunboats had pulled out to safety.

As he stood looking at the maddening scene and wondering how he would get back to his hospital in Wuchow, air-raid sirens rent the morning air and a mad rush ensued for shelter. Transfixed by the chaos, Bill watched the lethal planes roar into the harbor area. Red tracer bullets cut their way into boat after boat, leaving them in flames. With a start, he realized they were now spitting their fire at him, and he barely made the shelter of some freight boxes before the dock he was standing on was splintered by machine gun fire. Now he decided he did not need to go home that badly, and, running hard and low, he started back to the Hills' house.

When Eugene Hill and his wife returned from the seminary, bringing some vital records they hoped to protect, they found their late houseguest lying casually across a bed. Raising himself up on one elbow, he grinned and said, "You know, a guy could get killed out there."

Gene stated tersely, "The latest news bulletin says that the Japanese are just ten miles away. That means they are going to get here sometime tomorrow. You may be permanently assigned to this area—by the Japanese."

Louise Hill, ever effervescent and cheerful, quickly whipped up a lunch which reminded the two men that they still had appetites. Soon they were relaxed, despite the uncertainty of the morrow. Later on that afternoon, Gene finally convinced Louise of the expediency of going to Sha-Mein, and, borrowing the hospital car, he moved her to the apartment there.

The roar of guns and the incessant whine of airplanes awakened Bill and Gene before daylight the next morning. They drove to Sha-Mein to check on Mrs. Hill and to see if they could not find Bill transportation to Wuchow, but the docks were deserted. No boats could be seen anywhere on the river, and Bill, noticing a funny feeling in the pit of his stomach, realized he was not going anywhere.

To the northeast, the roar of big guns grew louder and on the horizon they could see an occasional flash of fire as the battle moved toward the city.

After watching the scene a moment, Bill said to Gene with a sigh of resignation, "Well, I guess this is obvious enough. Let's try to get back and see if we can help those people who are taking refuge in the hospital."

When they reached the hospital, they realized that when the battle for the city began, the hospital would be one of the safest places. Its subbasement was a bomb shelter and it would also protect its inhabitants from crossfire. Quickly, they formed a plan. The hospital basement could serve as a refugee center, but they must act immediately.

After arranging the subbasement to take care of about fifty people, Gene, Bill, and Dr. F. D. Woodward, who was also present for the executive committee meeting, moved through the area and enlisted the Christians there to help them gather their people and bring them to the hospital. They were urged to bring all the food they had, and extra clothes, and get to the hospital immediately.

Then, as if by an invisible telegraph, the Chinese knew that the lines had broken and the Japanese would soon be in their city. Panic set in and thousands of people started a great rush out of the burning city. The crush stopped the missionaries' progress and they took shelter in a side street, waiting for the stampeding crowd to clear. They witnessed one of the most horrible sights they had ever seen. In their panic, people began to trample one another in the headlong rush from the bombs and strafings. In places there was only blood, bone, and pulverized flesh to show those who had fallen.

After a lull, Bill and Gene took off in the hospital car, but soon were stopped by the crowds. A strafing run by a Japanese plane cleared the street for a moment, and Bill wheeled the car across the thoroughfare and past the area of congestion. Their drive back to the hospital was a hair-raising experience, and they finally decided to leave the car a couple of blocks away since it was such a ready target for machine guns. They had little time left, so they started toward the Hills' home for bedding and supplies. As they passed the seminary, they saw that it was now an armed bastion and a bloody battle was being fought there. A Chinese rear-guard group had commandeered the area to harass the oncoming Japanese forces. The Japanese were, in turn, pouring a withering fire into the little campus, and as the missionaries watched, they saw several of the defenders topple over.

Quickly, Bill and Gene skirted the campus, taking a low and sheltered road back to the Hills' house where a cache of canned food still lay untouched. At the Hills' house, they chucked four baskets full of canned goods into some bed sheets, and then, gathering up their bundles, started for the hospital. Eugene Hill, a strapping 200-pounder, had no trouble picking up his load and starting down the street, but Bill, a little over 140 pounds, had to abandon half his load before he got far. Praying the Japanese forces had not taken the seminary campus yet, they ran down the streets.

As the two missionaries, dogtrotting under their heavy loads, crossed the street below the seminary, they could see the Chinese soldiers abandoning their positions. When they reached an open square they had to cross to get to the hospital, the missionaries saw people running back and forth across the area to find last-minute shelter. They heard the rumble of Japanese tanks. In terrifying counterpoint, they heard the screams of people, the crackle of fire, and the whine of the overhead planes.

A Chinese running across the square spotted them and, calling Eugene Hill by name, ran toward them. "Pastor Hill! Pastor Hill,- save my life!" Ten feet away the man staggered and fell, dead. Within a few seconds a dozen people had fallen in front of the horror-stricken missionaries. Then they realized what was happening. They had stopped at the corner and thus were sheltered from a tank coming down the street to their right. There was no hope of getting back to the hospital now, and so Bill turned to Gene and said, "Let's turn back. We're going to get killed!"

Their repartee as they retraced their steps belied their fear. "Don't you want to go to heaven?" Gene asked.

The panting doctor replied, "Yes, but I didn't expect to get there today."

As they reached Gene's house, they dumped their packs in the hallway and dived for a nook behind the hall steps—plastering themselves as close to the floor as they could get.

No sooner had they taken cover than Japanese tanks, crunching through the streets, sprayed machine gun bullets against the house.

The exploding shells from the rumbling tanks and the bombs falling in the area shook loose the plaster that showered the two missionaries as they huddled on the floor.

After a moment's lull, Bill raised his head and whispered, "Gene, you all right? Do you think it is safe for us to go to the hospital?"

"I don't know; I'm afraid to look."

"I'm going to take a look," Bill said. On all fours he crawled down the entrance hall to the shattered door. Gently pulling it back, he peeked down the street—only to be greeted by the rumble of another tank and a din of fire. Scrambling, he barely had recovered shelter before another burst was fired into the residence. This time he and Gene lay there for a full fifteen minutes before either dared speak, much less move. (Days later, they counted thirty-eight bullet holes in the house.)

Cautiously, Gene moved to the door. The street was quiet and deserted. He summoned his friend, "If we're ever going to get to the hospital, we've got to go now."

Again they shouldered their loads and started into the streets, but the roar of still another tank convinced them they would never make it. There was nothing to do except drop the food and run.

Bill said, "Let's go! Every man for himself!"

Gene and Bill later wished they had timed the quarter-mile they ran from Gene's house to the hospital. Dodging the square this time, Gene turned the last corner before reaching the hospital and paused for a moment to look back. Bill Wallace was nowhere in sight. Panic seized the seminary teacher, and he started to return, sure that his friend had been caught in the withering crossfire. Just as he did, he saw Bill come around the corner, running for all he was worth, his arms flailing the air. Shells were hitting behind him, grazing the corner, but he was safe!

When the two arrived at the hospital, they found 268 refugees packed in the basement. Soon the wounded civilians and soldiers began pouring in, some walking, others being carried by friends or fellow soldiers—all stripped to their underwear for fear the Japanese would recognize them as soldiers and shoot them. The suffocating smell of humanity included not only the intangible odor of fear, but the very tangible stench of torn flesh and dried blood.

As Bill got his breath, he took charge of the wounded. With only the most meager of supplies, he began treating them—most of whom were suffering from shrapnel wounds. It was a bloody job.

Outside the hospital, Japanese tanks cruised back and forth broadcasting orders in Cantonese. They admonished the people to stay out of sight. Anyone in the streets would be shot.

Bill, not bothering to look up from his task, said, "He's not going to have to tell me twice!" As he worked, Gene Hill suddenly appeared at his side. "Where have you been?" asked Bill.

"I went upstairs to see if I could make a telephone call." Bill looked at him to see if he had gone mad. "I took a chance that the line was not yet down and I got a call in to the United Press office."

"What did they say?"

"They asked me how it was out here. When I said that the Japanese tanks were roaming the streets, they replied, 'Then it's all over. Canton has fallen.' "

It was Friday, October 21, 1938, 3:08 P.M.

Outside, unchecked fires illuminated the night sky. Inside, Bill worked by the aid of a flashlight to ease as much suffering as he could. Toward morning he decided he would have to operate on a young woman. Gene Hill managed to get a set of instruments from the operating room upstairs under cover of darkness, but they would have to wait for morning's light. Just before dawn her life ebbed away, and Bill Wallace bowed his head and sobbed with fatigue and sorrow.

The two men stayed in their basement shelter Saturday and Sunday. When they came out on Monday, the stench of death was everywhere. Few bodies had been removed. Boldly approaching the first Japanese soldiers, they showed their credentials and were allowed to pass.

The next day Bill went to the American consulate and arranged passage on a British gunboat that was leaving for Wuchow on Wednesday. The next two days were filled with efforts to get the hospital into shape for greater use.

An hour after Bill boarded the HMS *Robin* on Wednesday, a curfew was imposed on the city which would have prevented his leaving.

As the *Robin* steamed out of Canton harbor, Bill gave a big sigh and realized that, for nearly a week, he had not stopped to think about Wuchow or Knoxville or anything but the next moment and the task at hand. He had not even thought to notify the hospital that he was all right—a fact of which Dr. Beddoe was well aware. He wrote the Board in Richmond, Virginia:

"We at Wuchow are terribly worried about Dr. Wallace. He left here on the 16th for Canton for a meeting on the 18th. He has not returned to Wuchow. Two steamers have arrived from Canton, one leaving there on the 21st and one leaving there on the 22nd. These were British steamers and they brought out Chinese refugees. From radio reports the Japanese entered Canton on the 20th. We do not understand why Wallace sent no word. Also several passage boats from Canton have been bombed and sunk. We do not know what to think."

The whole staff at the Stout Memorial Hospital became alarmed when they heard nothing from Waa I Saang immediately after the fall of Canton. In the hospital chapel they prayed earnestly and tearfully for their beloved colleague. An hour later Dr. Beddoe received a message: "Arriving tomorrow on *Robin*. WALLACE."

7

The First Requisite

Bill Wallace stood on the porch of the hospital sipping an early morning cup of coffee and trying to clear the cobwebs from his mind. Sooner or later he was going to have to get some sleep, but there did not seem to be a place to stop. Every bed was filled; the emergency ward they had set up in the basement was dangerously overcrowded.

He saw Dr. Beddoe come out of the clinic, stethoscope in one hand and a bulging clipboard in the other. His sleeves were rolled up past his elbows and his collar was loose. It occurred to Bill that he did not often see Dr. Beddoe that informal. As Beddoe spotted him and came nearer, Bill noted the deep furrow to his brow and the dark circles under his eyes.

"I wonder if I'll ever smile again," the superintendent said absently as he daubed at the perspiration under his collar with a limp handkerchief. "Refugees keep coming and keep coming. I would not be surprised if ten thousand had come through here since Canton fell."

"I think we have most of them in the hospital," Bill said.

"I'm sure it seems like it," Beddoe replied and then, handing Bill the clipboard, said, "but we are going to have to find room for at least ten more. They can only survive with hospital treatment. We are having to treat and turn away people we would hospitalize in a moment, ordinarily."

Taking the clipboard, Bill said, "I'll see if we can clear ten more beds. There is not room for more pallets." Finishing his coffee, he started back into the hospital, then stopped and said, "When was it last 'ordinarily' around here?"

Beddoe shrugged. "I'm not sure I can remember." Looking down at the crowded clinic where a nurse was frantically beckoning him, he added, "The sights I have seen since then will take care of my nightmares for years to come."

Shortly after Bill had returned from Canton, Dr. Beddoe had called his staff together to consider the emergency. Japanese occupation was now a definite threat. Relating some of the sights Bill had seen in Canton, Beddoe told them he would understand if they chose to leave. To a person, they assured him they would stay by the job. The old missionary broke down and sobbed at their response, and the staff was deeply moved by this unusual display of emotion from the superintendent.

But staying by the job proved to be more difficult than anything they had yet faced. Each crisis before had made heavy demands for a while, but, in time, passed. The crisis precipitated by the hordes of refugees, however, had no ending.

The hospital was unable to keep accurate records in all the deluge of refugees. No one could remember how many operations Bill Wallace performed day and night. He became little more than skin and bones. At night the soft lights of the hospital reflected on his blood-spattered white coat as he moved through the crowded wards, attending the more serious of his patients— ordering medication for some whom he had seen during the day and examining others in preparation for surgery on the morrow.

With their sulfa and bandages, Bill, Dr. Beddoe, and the nurses were also administering the good news of Jesus Christ. The hospital evangelists and their helpers daily conducted services and experienced again and again the joy of not only seeing health and color return to the cheeks of their patients, but light and peace come into their lives.

Bill Wallace was a doctor; his basic ministry was one of healing. But he was in China first of all as a bearer of the good news of Jesus Christ, the glad tidings of forgiveness and eternal life inherent in the old, old message of God's love. Sometimes his soft, stuttering witness to that grace was more effective than the most eloquent evangelist's plea.

When Bill and Dr. Beddoe discussed how much longer their supplies and their physical strength could last in that constant pressure of human need, they realized things were changing. The Japanese were not advancing from Canton. With the strategic pocket around that city, they seemed content. They had control of all of China's industrial centers and leading ports as well as the main arteries of commerce. The three areas where foreign economic and commercial interests were heaviest were in their hands. The great river systems were now controlled by their forces of nearly 1,000,000 men. But the Chinese held on.

With a brief respite from war and its horrors, Bill Wallace's concerns became strictly provincial as he faced a job for which he had no appetite. Dr. and Mrs. Robert Beddoe had labored at Wuchow for six years with almost no relief. They needed a furlough. Dr. Wallace must serve as superintendent of the hospital for a year (1939).

Dr. Beddoe had come to the hospital at a time of crisis. By careful and prudent administration and single-minded effort he had brought it to a position of prominence, efficiency, and prestige. Now, Bill Wallace, his brilliant young colleague, was being recognized as a great surgeon throughout South China. Thanks to him, the people who had once looked on the hospital with disdain and spat out the epithet, "Foreign Devils," were looking with pride upon the Christian institution in their midst. They called it "The Life of China."

All of the misgivings Dr. Beddoe had harbored about Dr. Wallace's administrative abilities were focused on his own imminent departure. He left no stone unturned to render the hospital self-sufficient administratively. He set up a group of business managers and dismissed the student nurses. He reorganized the graduate nurses, ordered supplies for months ahead, and tried to anticipate every decision that could conceivably face Bill Wallace during the time he would be left in charge—a reluctant administrator.

Finally, bidding farewell to Bill Wallace and to Rex Ray, the only Southern Baptist missionaries left in Wuchow, Dr. and Mrs. Beddoe departed by a circuitous route for Hong Kong, the United States, and their beloved Texas. While Bill did not voice his feelings too readily, he admitted it was going to be a hard year. He was chief of staff, charged with a resident program, carrying a backbreaking surgery schedule, and now, hospital administrator.

Bill still had not learned to delegate responsibility. Soon the surprised staff realized that whether it was a plumbing fixture, a door hinge, or a complicated X-ray piece, the young doctor usually found time to do it himself rather than go through the channels of securing someone else. Actually, this was the way he liked to work. The mechanic in him came to the fore. And despite the fact that discipline was weak, bargaining less shrewd than it had once been, and billing neglected, the hospital work went on. In fact, it did right well.

Dr. Wallace came up one day when a hospital nurse was arguing with two orderlies about the removal of a body. Highly superstitious and convinced that such work was coolie labor, the orderlies were refusing the task. Dr. Wallace caught the drift of the conversation, picked up the body in his arms, and then walked past the open-mouthed orderlies, down to the morgue. It was the last time a Stout Memorial orderly ever refused to carry a body. If the great doctor could do this, surely it was not beneath them! Drawn by the winsomeness of the doctor's humility and dedication, the Chinese followed him in a way which enabled the hospital to do an excellent job.

Bill worked hard that year (1940) to carry on all his assignments. Somebody wrote to Dr. Maddry in Richmond that Bill was at a breaking point physically and mentally under the burden of his responsibilities at Wuchow. Whether someone traveling through the area had become alarmed at the fantastic pace the lean physician kept, or whether it was somebody personally reacting to the laissez-faire way he worked, or whether someone had made a statement that was simply misunderstood, is not known. At any rate, Dr. Maddry became so concerned that he immediately wired Dr. Beddoe, who was speaking in Florida, and asked him to check the story and then prepare to return to China at the earliest possible moment.

Two weeks later Dr. Beddoe received the longest letter he had ever received from Bill Wallace:

"Everything is going along peacefully in Wuchow. I expect when you get this letter, you will be packing up to come back, and we certainly need you. I am a bad manager and a bad financier. I am afraid you did not get much satisfaction from my list of drugs, but it is very hard to say what you need for a year in advance. However, the list we sent you constitutes the main drugs in amounts which we used this year. It'll be a good idea to bring some rubber gloves, hot water bottles, and sheets also. Perhaps in light of some inquiries, I should also say I have never felt better or been happier in my whole life than I am right now."

Another letter from one of the office workers and still another one from missionary Rex Ray confirmed that Dr. Wallace was not only holding up well under his responsibility, but was actually thriving under it. Bill Wallace was happiest ministering to the needs of people, doing the work for which he felt called, and for which he had diligently trained himself. The busier and more demanding the times, the greater was his sense of fulfilment. Though he undoubtedly felt the strain of five long years in China, and especially with this year of added responsibility, he was definitely in his element.

To his pleasure, Dr. Beddoe found the hospital full and prospering when he returned to Wuchow in July, 1940. Except for the growing problem of supplies, due to the Japanese blockade, the hospital stood strong and sure—a lighthouse in the middle of a stormy sea. It was obvious to the sharp eye of the older missionary that the reluctant young administrator had done a magnificent job.

Now it was Bill's time to return to the United States for a well-earned furlough. The hospital staff hated to see him go at a time when he was so desperately needed. Yet, they realized his plans to spend a year in advanced surgical studies would make him even more valuable to the Stout Memorial Hospital.

Several of his colleagues wrote to the Board shortly after he departed for the States, expressing their appreciation of him. Their letters told what kind of trial term the young missionary had had:

"There is no overstating the value of Dr. Wallace's work. . . . No words of mine could overpraise him."

"Dr. Wallace has a brilliant future in China. His fame will travel over an entire nation, distinction he could hardly expect to attain in America."

"He might be called Silent Bill, for he is a man of few words, but brave deeds. Words may vanish into thin air, but deeds never die. It was the deed on the Cross that saved the world."

"What Dr. Wallace did during his first term of service in China—the trial term—will bear fruit down through the years."

"As a physician he possesses, to a greater degree than any man I have ever known, the first requisite—that of staying by the job at hand till the heavens fall and though all hope seems to be lost."

"If you want to find him, find the sickest patient in the hospital, and there he will be."

Bill Wallace was unaware of the accolades preceding him. He was heading home. The blue of the Pacific and the peaceful nights at sea were turning his thought from his adopted country to his native land. His thoughts were now of Knoxville and friends and the Tennessee hills. He was anticipating a year of study and renewed friendships with a consuming eagerness. His trial term was behind him; he had already evaluated it and summed it up:

"When I get back home, I don't know how I will stack up as far as my profession is concerned. Had I been in America, I could always have gone to an older doctor and asked him how to do certain operations, but I was the only surgeon there. No, I don't know how I will stack up as far as my profession is concerned, but I can say this, I know the Lord Jesus Christ better than I did five years ago."

An Edge for the Blade

The countryside flashed by the window like an accelerated movie as the train rumbled eastward. Mountains, desert, canyons, plains, and woods took their turn onstage. Bill Wallace drank it in, as only a man with an enormous thirst for home-sights could.

He noticed that his clothes were a bit out of style, and snatches of conversation convinced him he was going to need a lot of language reorientation. Even colloquialisms had changed. He laughed out loud at the words of a popular song. The scene was both strange and familiar. Often he was engaged in conversation.

"So you are a missionary in China. I hear it's pretty rough out there."

"At times. But the Chinese are holding their own now."

"Well, I figure Germany's our problem, anyhow. Those Japs are just scrap iron merchants; we've nothin' to worry about there."

Remembering Canton, Bill smiled silently. No use trying to convince the man otherwise. The past three weeks had made the whole adventure seem a bit unreal, anyway. The present dominated his thinking. He tried to recall Wuchow, the hospital, the Beddoes, Dr. Leung, Nurse Luk, but they were already receding beneath more recent scenes: Hong Kong; Shanghai and the strange sensation of being in the midst of the Japanese without having to jump for cover; Honolulu; San Francisco; the memories ahead toward which his thoughts raced more swiftly than the rail-bound streamliner. In his mind's eye he was seeing Knoxville and Broad Street, the old homeplace and Ruth Lynn and Syd. They were becoming clear again after having been so dim through the years in China.

61

"What makes a doctor spend his life in a place like China?"

His dinner companion's question brought him back to the moment.

"Don't misunderstand me; I admire you for it. I just wonder why."

Bill smiled, "I guess each person's reasoning is, in a sense, unique, but my reason is simple enough. When I was trying to decide what I should do with my life, I became convinced that God wanted me to be a medical missionary. That decision took me to China. And that, along with the fact that I was extremely happy there, will take me back." He paused for a moment, a little uneasy before his companion's obvious admiration. "I'm not going back because I'm heroic. Actually, I'm a coward. But I want to go back because it's where I'm supposed to be."

The man, a successful business executive, was silent, lost in his own thoughts. Then, turning to the candid, clear-eyed missionary, he said, "You make me wonder if I have not missed something down the line."

"Knoxville! Knoxville!" The familiar cry of the conductor was unnecessary. For two hours Bill Wallace had been aware of the East Tennessee countryside. He had reveled in each successive scene, marked the new, remembered the old.

And then he was home. Ruth Lynn and Syd Stegall were there to greet him. For a few moments they all talked at once, laughing at their lack of direction, only glad to be together again.

On the way home, Bill had them drive him about Knoxville so he could see the city of his youth and behold the changes. The cars enthralled him. The magazines had kept him abreast of most model changes, but here they were, sleek and shiny, all of them.

They drove by the old home on the corner of Broadway and Silver and stopped across the street. Bill just looked. A lot of memories rushed back. He wished for a moment he could see patients walking into the downstairs entrance, or the lean figure of his father emerge with candy for a child, stethoscope dangling from his neck. The nostalgia was strong, but it made him aware of how much time had passed since his departure five years earlier.

Bill's brother-in-law had built a new home on the north side of Knoxville. It was to become Bill's "permanent address." He loved the place, with its big trees and broad, sloping lawn. He exclaimed over the brick patio with its barbecue pit. A breezeway he claimed for himself and christened as a sleeping porch. That evening they sat under the trees and talked.

At first Ruth Lynn and Sydney plied Bill with questions, but before they knew it, they found themselves doing the talking, filling him in on things that had happened while he was gone. He had skilfully and characteristically turned the conversation from himself.

Two days after his arrival he was walking the wooded slopes of the Smoky Mountains near Gatlinburg. Memories can become exhausted over the years, and as he walked, he was conscious of the need to refuel for the years ahead. With senses alert, he took in the haze of the mountains, the green of the hickories, the laurel, the stately pines, and the broad-leaf maples. The bright, sparkling waters of the creeks splashing across the rocks lifted his spirits.

Everyone wanted to see him. Friends and relatives invited him for dinners and vainly tried to get him to talk about China and the bombings and the war. They ended up talking about themselves and what they had done during the last five years.

The chief bane of his furlough was that everyone wanted him to speak, and he declared he would rather go through a Japanese air raid than do so. He knew people wanted him to relive his experiences, to dramatize them; it was difficult for him even to share the basic facts. The blood, destruction, hunger, and suffering of China were a long way off. He was not one to live in the past. China's needs continued to live in his daily prayers, but he had laid them aside for the present.

Bill did make two speeches. The first one was made that summer before a woman's group. One day before the meeting, Ruth Lynn peered out of her kitchen window and saw him walking back and forth over the green yard, agonizing over what he would say. From time to time he leaned against a tree and, with painfully self-conscious gestures, mumbled the words of his tediously prepared speech. No one was more aware than Bill Wallace that when God passed out gifts, public speaking was not one of those that came his way. He managed to dodge most speech-making, and at church he got away with just speaking to people individually and smiling at them. They did all the talking.

During his furlough he decided to reactivate his social life, which had suffered badly during the hectic years in China. While he did not return home with the express purpose of marrying, his close friends in China knew he had not totally rejected the idea. Within a week he had made a few contacts with girls who liked to talk and ride and eat (his idea of a good time), and he was enjoying himself.

Bill realized that a furlough was a time for renewal, but he also saw it as a God-given opportunity to hone to a new sharpness whatever ability he had as a surgeon. The fires and tribulations of China had tempered the blade; he had come home to put an edge on it.

He originally planned to study in Europe in one of the celebrated centers of medical research. The war and Nazi aggression put an end to that. He read his medical journals avidly, even in China, and from his reading decided that the University of Pennsylvania's postgraduate course in surgery would be the best investment of his time. He had asked Sydney to enrol for him even before he returned to the States. Additional research turned up the fact that he could take still another short course in X-ray at Harvard University during the three months he would have left when he completed his work at the University of Pennsylvania.

This was the ambitious schedule he had outlined, and within a few days after his return, he was eagerly anticipating the experience.

In late August Bill received a wire from the Foreign Mission Board in Richmond, asking him if he would attend Ridgecrest Baptist Assembly in North Carolina and give his testimony. He could stop over on his way to Philadelphia, they reasoned. The desire to visit again the beautiful assembly grounds in the heart of the Blue Ridge Mountains overcame the unpleasant prospects of another speaking engagement. He wired his acceptance. As it turned out, he was very glad he did, because he met a delightful young woman who greatly piqued his interest.

As an employee of the Foreign Mission Board, she had long known of the young doctor who was fast becoming a legend. In fact, she was present when he attended the assembly just before his appointment in 1935 and remembered very clearly that experience: He was tall and slender, with clear complexion and blue eyes—standing against the whiteness of the main building. She was introduced to him then, and along with many others, she wondered if he would marry the young woman he had brought with him. Later, when he had not done so, she wondered why, though she was secretly glad.

This time there was no one with him and the introduction "took." Soon they were sitting together in the sessions and walking about the grounds. This did not go unnoticed by whispering friends and colleagues. She teased him about the young ladies who asked him for his autograph. And they talked of China. Her parents had served there as missionaries, and she—she could go Bill one better—she had been born there.

The night he spoke, she sat quietly in the back of the auditorium and agonized with him through his message. It wasn't that he spoke badly. She just knew, instinctively, how he was suffering. Knowing of his incredible experiences, she desperately wanted him to be able to share the drama of them with his listeners. Instead, he spoke simply and matter-of-factly. He was totally unable to call attention to himself. She hoped the audience would respond to him anyway, for she sensed that, even in his reticence, they were hearing one of God's really choice apostles. Yes, she decided, they did realize and appreciate him. But few people would remember him as a speaker.

"I hope I see you again," he said to her when the week was over.

"You ought to come by Richmond, you know," she replied, a twinkle in her eyes. "After all, that's the home office."

"You're right! I really ought to visit the home office."

September found Bill hard at work in University of Pennsylvania's postgraduate course in surgery. He settled into his new surroundings with great satisfaction, relishing the whiteness and preciseness of the scientific atmosphere. Like a man with an unquenchable appetite, he launched himself into intensive study. He took only widely spaced respites for sight-seeing and brief visits with friends. He spent most of his time outside the prescribed routine observing surgery, browsing through the vast medical archives available to him, and discussing new techniques with some of the advanced men in the field. More than once, as he worked or heard a lecture or observed an operation, a scene from China would return to his mind: he would view again a patient that perhaps now he could help, and he would quietly thank God for his opportunity.

Shortly before Christmas, Bill received a long letter from Dr. Charles Maddry, executive secretary of the Foreign Mission Board, inviting him to be his guest in Richmond over the holidays. It was a windfall for Bill for two reasons. First, Dr. Maddry presented a thousand dollars to him from some Texas women who had raised it to help him with his expenses. And Bill sorely needed help. He had exhausted his insurance savings in his fall expenses. While he had never really expected to have any problem enrolling in his spring and summer course, he wondered after the money came what he would have done without it.

Of course, the second reason he considered the invitation a windfall was that it gave him a chance to renew his friendship with the young lady he had met at Ridgecrest. Associates did not accuse Dr. Maddry of being Cupid, but they did point out that the administrator could just as easily have mailed the thousand dollars to Bill.

Wallace met the young lady's family and had several meals in their home. After the meals, they sat around a crackling fire and talked of China. Bill listened raptly as they told of their experiences in his adopted land. Then he filled in for them details on the latest developments in the place where they had spent their lives. It was not all family fellowship. The two young people took in the sights of historic old Richmond and managed long walks. It became a flourishing friendship before Bill returned to Philadelphia.

Now he was torn three ways. First, he was corresponding regularly with his young friend in Richmond and found his thoughts following his letters more and more. Second, he was entranced by his study at the university and believed that giving it anything less than his best was spiritual disobedience. Third, bad feeling between the United States and Japan began to cause him some concern about his re-entry into China, and the growing crisis around the world was causing Uncle Sam to begin drafting many doctors.

Meanwhile, Dr. Beddoe had heard about the new draft law enacted in the United States and the shortage of doctors. He wrote Dr. Maddry to take all measures to make sure Dr. Wallace was exempted so that he could return to Wuchow. Dr. Maddry tried to reassure him:

"The State Department has ruled that if we can show that a single missionary is essential to a particular work in China, and to a work that is already begun, he or she may go back. Therefore, I don't think we will have any trouble when his year of furlough is over; although, the Government may catch him in the dragnet of the draft and we may not be able to send him."

That statement reassured Dr. Beddoe like one of the sugar-pills the hospital used from time to time.

Bill finished his work in Philadelphia in late spring and, after a brief visit in Knoxville, entrained to Boston and Harvard, where he began his special studies in roentgenology. Again, the opportunity to work in an advanced medical center and in association with some of the really brilliant minds in medicine thrilled him.

He remembered his old friend Dr. Dewey Peters's admonition, "Always practice the best medicine." He realized with satisfaction that, because of his furlough opportunities, he was going to be able to practice a lot better medicine when he returned to Wuchow.

Early in July, while Bill was in school at Harvard, Ruth Lynn and Sydney proposed that they meet him in New York for a week-

end vacation. Bill agreed, with one stipulation: that he be allowed
to invite his friend from Richmond. They were wondering if at
long last "William" was about to take a bride.

"It would be kind of cruel," jested Sydney, "if Bill Wallace's
heart, so long sought after by female missionaries in the Orient,
was stolen away by a home office employee."

The group had a delightful time in New York. They laughed
uproariously at a matinee performance of *Panama Hattie,* took in
Coney Island, the Staten Island Ferry, the Empire State Building,
and many other New York tourist sights. Before an off-Broadway
pizza shop, Bill entertained them by pantomiming the deft manipu-
lations of the pizza-maker inside.

"I believe William is becoming an extrovert," Ruth Lynn whispered to the approving Sydney.

Despite their efforts to hold on to every moment of it, the brief
vacation ended. The morning they left New York, Bill came up
with the idea that he would possibly do better to drive with them
to some point in New Jersey and then catch a train to Boston.
"After all, it would enable me to miss the New York crowds at the
station, and you know how I hate crowds."

Each time they came to a station as they drove South, Bill turned
it down and suggested they drive to the next one. "This place looks
a little small." They drove another ten miles or so. "I doubt if I
could get a good magazine there." Further down the line, "That
place doesn't look too clean." And on it went, to everyone's entertainment. But his motives were not entertainment. He hated to let
them go. With great reluctance, he finally boarded the train.

There was still no talk of marriage. Bill and the girl were good
friends and they enjoyed being with one another.

He finished his course of study at Harvard and realized it was
time to return to China. He had time for a few days in Knoxville
and then he would have to leave for San Francisco—provided his
visa and passage came through. When he stopped in New York to
change trains for Knoxville, however, it occurred to him that it
would be very little out of the way to go through Richmond. On
an impulse he climbed on the southbound train to Richmond.

At Richmond's Main Street station, a quick trip to a phone booth brought the disappointing discovery that the girl had left the day before for a vacation with her family in the western part of the state. Studying time schedules frantically, the determined young doctor figured out a way he could stop off at Roanoke and still make Knoxville in time to get packed and on his way. On the phone again, he spent for long distance calls an amount that he would not later reveal when Sydney teased him about it. He finally located the girl and asked her to meet him at the station in Roanoke.

A few hours later she was driving him through the Blue Ridge Mountains toward her family's summer cottage. They spent three delightful days together. They took long walks on the winding paths, relishing the beauty of the multicolored algae-cushioned trails, the fruit-laden vines, and the almost tropical lushness of the summer growth. They spent a lot of time talking. One day Bill found a large bone, probably from a deer that perished in the forest in days gone by. He said, with mock seriousness, "Now this is a beautiful tibia." As they continued their walk, he talked about the future of China missions. With the ridiculous-looking bone he made exaggerated gestures to accompany each point. She laughed and was amazed at this rather unexpected side of her friend.

"You know what really scares me about going back to China this time?" he asked. "It's not the Japanese nor the possibility of the whole Pacific becoming embroiled in a war. Not really. The thing that really scares me is that Dr. Beddoe is getting near retirement, and that when he leaves, the Foreign Mission Board will expect me to run that place. Now that really bothers me. I'm not fit to run even a sidewalk lemonade stand. I've got about as much business sense as this bone." With that he lifted the bone in a grandiose gesture.

"How in the world can they expect a doctor to run an establishment like that?" he continued. "Oh, I grant you, now and then a man like Beddoe comes along who is a born administrator. But most doctors, like me, are not cut out for that. I want to practice 'good medicine.' Do you know what that means? That means I've got to be on my toes constantly, keeping up with new medicines, experiments, surgical innovations, and new findings on old problems. Not to mention the fact that if a fellow's going to practice 'good medicine,' he's going to need every moment of his time to supervise tests, study histories, examine, and—well—just practice medicine."

Realizing that she was seeing her missionary friend in a rare mood, the young lady smiled demurely, but did not speak.

"How in the world can a man practice medicine when he's got to spend all his time worrying about hospital supplies, janitorial procedures, mechanical problems, disciplinary action, hiring and firing, and all that goes with it? A hospital like the Stout Memorial Hospital needs a business manager."

He stopped and turned to look at her. Their path had led them to a grassy meadow that sloped down through delicate dogwoods and leafy maples, scattered hickories, and stately pines. The hills that separated them from the Shenandoah shimmered in the sunlight. Bill Wallace was totally oblivious to it. The girl listened.

"I'm not running the Foreign Mission Board, I realize, but I figure you're the nearest I'll get to the people who do run it, and so I'll tell you. We need to start thinking about appointing more laymen to do jobs that preachers are just not prepared to do.

"Why not find good Christian businessmen, trained and experienced in their fields, to come to places like Wuchow? A fellow like that would be worth more than a doctor. I know that's a sinful statement even to say, but it's true.

"And why not appoint builders? Missions is a team job. I just fill one little gap, and I am only a doctor. Preachers ought to have responsibility of preaching and beginning churches, and instead we ask them to manage everything and to act in all kinds of capacities."

The look on her face stopped him and he laughed at himself. "Well, I'm really carrying on, am I not?"

"I like to hear you express yourself. I didn't know you felt so strongly about these things. But you're right; I'm not running the Foreign Mission Board."

"Well, you tell those people who do run it another thing for me, will you? I met a wonderful doctor at Harvard who is a Southern

Baptist and wants to go to the mission field, and I don't think our Board's going to appoint him. Now, that's a fine thing. Some Board will appoint him. Why don't we?"

She was quiet again.

With a sly smile he said, "Well, I admit I hope they don't send him to our station, as he does have a few angles."

With a flip of his wrist, the bone sailed out into the meadow and with it Bill Wallace's plan for renovating missionary strategy.

The subject of marriage did not come up. He had already told his sister he was fond of his friend. "I really ought to marry her, and I am not sure why I don't. But as I've said before, how can you take a girl to China at a time like this? There's a war going on." And that was it.

When she saw him off at the railroad station, he asked her to write, said he would see her in a few years, and boarded his train.

As the Virginia countryside receded, he was not thinking back. He was looking ahead. He had set his course and all that was in him was a moving, urging force toward China.

9

The Mantle of Leadership

Dr. Robert Beddoe sat down and placed his hands on the familiar typewriter keys. He began to type furiously. He was worried and he habitually worked out his anxieties in correspondence. Such work took the edge from the anxieties, even if it made for volatile correspondence. Suddenly he stopped, reached for a soiled, ragged-edged map of South China, and laboriously began to refigure the route of his colleague's journey from America.

Bill Wallace had sailed from San Francisco on August 14 and arrived in Hong Kong on September 3. Dr. Beddoe had received definite word that Bill flew to Shiukwan on September 16. From there he should have been able to make Luichow easily and Luichow was only three days away from Wuchow. Thirteen days had elapsed, for it was now the 29th.

Running his hand across his head and pushing aside the papers, Dr. Beddoe rifled his memory for related events that could account for Bill's delay in arrival. Shiukwan was bombed on the 18th, but Bill should have been out of there before then. Could that Japanese raiding party have cut off the Luichow Road at the time Bill was on it? Growing apprehension caused him to turn again to his typing.

"Dr. Wallace is somewhere upcountry. He is very sparing of words and does not acquaint one with his movements in places and he is sorely needed. . . ."

Four days later, on October 3, Bill still had not arrived, but word came that he had left Shiukwan safely.

"You would think he would have the sense to know we're worried!" Dr. Beddoe fumed.

Chapel service on the morning of October 6 was given entirely to impassioned prayers on behalf of Waa I Saang. The degree of the staff's concern was evidenced by an emotional outburst from

72

one of the nurses: "He is dead! I know he is dead!" It emphasized the gloom that was settling over the waiting staff.

The next day a dusty, bedraggled American climbed painfully from a pedicab in front of the Baptist clinic. As the driver shuffled off with his rickety vehicle, the man stood for a moment looking at the clinic before him and the hospital that towered behind it. His look was that of a man drinking in a sight he had not really expected to see again. Then, picking up a worn bag, he walked up the steps, and unconsciously precipitated a celebration that rivaled the Chinese New Year.

"Waa I Saang is back!" The cry echoed across the hospital yard and was relayed in seconds to every ward in the five-story building.

Dr. Beddoe, hearing the news, breathed a fervent prayer of thanks. Then he rushed out to greet Bill, though he reminded himself that his reticent surgeon had caused him a lot of anxiety by not wiring his whereabouts. But, when he saw the grinning, slender figure surrounded by laughing, weeping, chattering staff members, he forgot all about his worries. Bill, seeing the blinking administrator, knew he was welcome.

That night at supper Bill talked matter-of-factly of the strange and miraculous odyssey that had brought him on a circuitous route from Shiukwan. With Japanese planes harassing all traffic, and especially railroad traffic, the trains ran only at night, if they ran at all. To get back to Wuchow, Bill tried bus, train, car, and even walking. More than once he jumped for cover as Japanese planes roared down from the China skies, their wings spitting death. He related frantic efforts to claw a hole in the mud-and-water-filled ditches to find cover.

Once his train remained in a mountain tunnel all day to avoid Japanese planes which were lying in wait for it. Another time he and his fellow travelers abandoned a bus and made for cover as Japanese troops, striking deep into Free China territory to forage for supplies, cut off the road. The story could have been told heroically, but before Bill had finished, he had his hearers laughing.

"Bill, we thought you would bring somebody back with you from the States. You know we got some rather interesting letters

from people who saw you from time to time." Mrs. Beddoe noticed
with satisfaction that Bill blushed at her remarks.

"Now, Mrs. Beddoe, you know it's not safe to bring a woman
to China at a time like this. And besides, who would have me?"

Mrs. Beddoe, laughing, said, "I can name several who would if
you would stop running long enough to let them catch you."

Within a few days Bill felt as if he had never left Wuchow.
Caught up in the routine of the work, he settled himself into the
China scene, warmly aware that he was more comfortable than
ever. This was his home.

His reputation as a surgeon did not suffer while he was gone and
upon returning he once again began his marathon schedule. He
was performing operations by 6:30 on most mornings and did not
pause for breakfast until around midmorning. Then, he usually ate
it—a piece of bread and a glass of milk—as he took steps, two at a
time, from surgery, to ward, to office. He was on call at all times
and often visited the hospital several times during the night. He
indulged his patients to a fault, giving them just what was asked
unless some principle was involved. He tried always to make sure
that every patient was the recipient of "good medicine."

In the meantime, the stalemate in China was provoking the
Japanese to new, bolder moves. Then came Pearl Harbor.

America was planning to strengthen her island bases in the
Pacific and especially the Philippines, but she had not been able to
do it substantially before the Japanese struck at a strategic time.
Their far-flung maneuvers met with startling success. Hong Kong,
Manila, Singapore, all fell before conquering Japanese armies.

This had an immediate effect upon Wuchow. It reduced the
outlets Free China had with the rest of the world. Hong Kong was
their closest door and their gateway to the rest of the world, and now
Hong Kong was in Japanese hands. Indochina was falling to the
Japanese and the Burma Road was a risky and limited corridor.

The closing off of Hong Kong brought severe supply problems.
Food and medicines were more and more difficult to find. Fortunately, there was nothing the indefatigable "cowboy missionary"
from Texas, Rex Ray, loved more than the adventure of running

the Japanese blockade for desperately needed medical supplies. They were not always easy to get, but in countless dangerous and sometimes humorous adventures, Ray came home with the "bacon."

Inflation was dealing the missionaries misery also. Bill commissioned Rex to find some sulfa drugs at any price. Ray brought back a bottle of 1,000 tablets. Price, $3,250, Hong Kong dollars. When he brought them in apologetically, Bill said, "Forget it, Rex, that's just money. These tablets mean lives. Remember, there's no price tag on life."

The bombs came as before.

On their way to the shelter another day, one of the women missionaries said to Bill, "I am getting so nervous, I don't know what I'll do."

Bill smiled and said, "We'll do what God wants us to do. It doesn't make any difference what happens to us. The only important thing is that when it does happen, we be found doing the will of God."

The problems of carrying on missionary work in Free China while it was largely cut off from the Western world and its source of supply became increasingly difficult. The Foreign Mission Board hoped to alleviate the difficulty somewhat by asking Dr. Robert Beddoe to take on responsibility as Board representative for the whole area. Also Dr. Beddoe took upon himself the responsibilities of the hospital in Kweilin. He soon realized that wearing three hats is no easy job for any man, and that the only thing to do was to turn his Wuchow responsibilities over to Bill Wallace. He would then move his own headquarters to Kweilin.

Bill Wallace would not talk about it. Every time Dr. Beddoe brought up the subject, he simply said, "I will not accept the administrative responsibility of this hospital, and that's all there is to it." Beddoe was at a loss to understand Bill's attitude.

It is hard to imagine two more different people than Bill Wallace and Robert Beddoe. Beddoe was a born administrator, and his almost over-solicitous protection of Bill to allow the younger doctor to give himself wholly to the ministry of medicine had greatly eased the young man's adjustment to the mission field.

In turn, Bill deeply loved the Beddoes, regarding them almost as a son regards his parents. As far as communication goes, he was much closer to Mrs. Beddoe, who made sure that his housekeeper took adequate care of him and looked after his personal needs—repairing shirts, mending socks, altering clothes.

But Bill found it difficult to communicate with Dr. Beddoe. They did much better on a feeling level, understanding each other's attitudes without need to discuss them. When things were brought into the open, the two men sometimes had trouble. Thus it was, that when Dr. Beddoe approached Bill about taking over the administrative responsibilities of the hospital to release him to go to Kweilin, the surgeon's refusal to do so completely frustrated the older missionary.

The problem was aggravated when Rex Ray moved to Shiuchow and asked Bill to take over the job as station treasurer. Bill refused with considerable emphasis. When Dr. Beddoe heard about it, he accused Bill of unwillingness to assume his share of the general mission burden and reminded him that in times like this everybody had to accept extra responsibility.

In the early fall of 1943 Bill, usually the picture of health, began to lose strength. An infected tooth had poisoned his system, and he suffered from lack of rest necessitated by the continuous effort demanded at the hospital. Realizing that should Bill become physically disabled, the situation would be tragic, Dr. Beddoe reluctantly abandoned his idea and continued to carry on from Wuchow.

When Bill's health began to improve, Dr. Beddoe decided to take matters into his own hand. Bill came out of surgery one morning to find Dr. Beddoe supervising the removal of his office from the hospital to his home.

Puzzled, Bill asked, "What's up, Doctor?"

"As of tonight, I am severing all relationship with this hospital. I will carry on my other responsibilities from the house." With that Beddoe picked up a file of letters and walked right past his surgeon. As an afterthought, he added, "Bill, you can either run this hospital or let it fall apart. I'm doing what I have to do."

From his porch a few moments later, Beddoe saw Bill walking up the path from the hospital with a look of deep concern on his face. When he entered the room, he said simply to Beddoe, "I will never accept the superintendency of this hospital as long as you are in China."

Beddoe was completely taken aback. It cut across all that he knew and believed about his fellow worker. Checking his urge to voice a sharp retort, it occurred to him that maybe something was involved that he had not seen before.

"Bill, I don't understand your attitude. Is it based on reasons that you have not shared with me? Tell me why you feel that way."

"It's hard to put into words, but I see this as *your* hospital. You built it. You saved it when it was on the brink of financial disaster. You've given your life here. Everyone respects you. The whole tone of the hospital is built around you. I don't believe this hospital should be taken from you."

Dr. Beddoe was amazed. Why had he not seen it before? Bill felt that the Board was asking him to give up something he wanted in order to carry responsibilities he did not want, and that if he, Bill, refused to take them on, the Board would allow Dr. Beddoe to stay. Bill had been thinking of him all along.

"I'm sorry I've been too dumb to see why you didn't want me to go, Bill. The Board's not taking the hospital away from me; I feel that this new work is a responsibility that I have been uniquely prepared for, and I want to take it. After the emergency is over, I can come back to the hospital until time for my retirement. Would you accept the responsibility if we ask the Board to agree to the term 'temporary'?"

Bill brightened. "Why, yes, I would accept it under those conditions. I will take over as long as you remain administrator and as long as I am regarded as simply temporary superintendent, as I was on your last furlough."

Telling his wife about the conversation, Dr. Beddoe broke down. The depth of Bill's loyalty to him was something he had not realized, and the correct old missionary wept unashamedly.

With fear and trembling, Bill Wallace assumed the responsibility of running the complex institution. Despite his experience in 1939, it was painful going. The war had so complicated the situation that administration took more and more of his time. When it came to a choice between an administrative matter and a patient's need, the decision was not difficult to make. This did not ease the situation, however, and within a few months, Dr. Beddoe wrote the Board's secretary in Richmond, "Poor Wallace. He is in a half-dozen pots of hot water already. It may be necessary to get some nonmedical man to take over the administration of the hospital."

And what problems they had at the hospital! Some of the student nurses, hoping to get away from the tensions of the hospital, attended an all-night dancing party. It caused a near riot among the evangelistic workers of the hospital who felt that all discipline had broken down with Beddoe's leaving. In the past this would have been handled quickly and firmly by Dr. Beddoe, but to everyone's dismay and uncertainty, Bill acted as if it had never happened.

A few weeks after this Dr. Beddoe received a telegram from Wuchow saying that a dispute had arisen in the church and he must come immediately to settle it lest it erupt in a complete breakdown of the local Chinese Baptist organization. Dr. Beddoe, deciding that Bill was going to have to sink or swim, forwarded the telegram to him with a note. "This is your responsibility now."

This was almost too much for Bill. It was hard enough to take over the hospital. Responsibility for the work of the entire Wuchow station was more than he had bargained for. He was not a Dr. Beddoe; he could not function like Dr. Beddoe; the sooner people quit expecting it of him, the better off he would be.

This whole period may be looked upon as one of the most severe crises of his missionary career, but he stuck it out. He worked out his own system of administration, and by early 1944, his leadership was established. The station could not have been more tranquil.

The changed spirit began with the corps of doctors and nurses and hospital staff members who had already become passionately loyal. It expanded to the evangelistic workers who had always revered Dr. Wallace, but now had come to respect him as a man of judgment and leadership. Dr. Wallace's leadership was in terms of his own example and his own dedication, and it took a little longer to take hold than if it had been exercised from an authoritarian framework.

In early 1944, the hospital enjoyed the most effective evangelistic thrust it had experienced during all the war years. In the Wuchow church, where Bill served as a deacon, the people began to realize that he was not only a skilled doctor, but a dedicated churchman who was one of them. The result was that they accepted more leadership in their own right with remarkable success. Before, they had expected most matters to be decided by the senior missionary on the field.

The mantle of leadership had fallen upon the reluctant doctor. In the power of the Lord Jesus Christ, he emerged sufficient for the day.

One of the by-products of the responsibilities that had been thrust upon Bill was increased participation in the community at large. Before, he had entrusted the city, public relations, and all of the attendant problems to Dr. Beddoe, content to perform his own particular ministry. Now he found himself active in the Wuchow Rotary Club, visiting the homes of Wuchow citizens for meals, attending civic functions, and participating in civic affairs as a consultant to the city fathers. This was the new Bill Wallace, the man whose advice and judgment were as valuable as his healing skills.

Also, he found a widening circle of friends among the other missionaries in the area. On the hill that rose from the peninsula between the West and Fu Rivers, stood the Christian and Missionary Alliance station. There Dr. William C. Newbern headed up a very effective group of dedicated missionaries. Since Bill was the only Baptist missionary left at Wuchow, he was often invited to "the Hill" for Sunday dinner and after a while it became a standing invitation. Sunday mornings after church would find Bill hurrying to finish his rounds at the hospital. Then he would walk into Wuchow to purchase a chicken and, swinging it unceremoniously by the neck, journey to "the Hill" whistling softly with anticipation of visiting his friends.

The nearby Maryknoll mission had long depended on the Stout Memorial Hospital for its medical care, but no close relationships had ever developed between the Catholic missionaries and the Protestant groups. Now, to their surprise, Bill not only treated them when they came to the hospital, but visited the mission to follow up on their care and well-being. All their efforts to pay him came to no avail, nor did their insistence that he not trudge all the way out to their station just to treat one of them.

The result was that Bill "belonged" to all the missionaries of the area. Despite theological differences, he found with them a sense of brotherhood in Christ that transcended all barriers. Indeed, the differences seemed petty in his presence.

This was the man God fashioned for an incredible task.

10

A Pillar of Fire by Night

Daily, Bill Wallace hovered over his radio set, listening to reports of the Japanese advance, and plotted their course on a worn map of China.

The Japanese had begun an all-out offensive in the late spring of 1944 in a last-ditch effort to ward off the specter of doom taking shape with their reversals in the South Pacific. Despite the growing air superiority of the Americans in China, Stilwell's progress in Burma, and draining resources, their effort threatened to break China's back.

Bill reviewed the meaning of the marks on his map: from a staging area in the Yangtze Valley around Hankow, the Japanese had effected a pincer's movement against the starving Honan Province. After liquidating a Chinese army of three hundred thousand, they turned south toward the great Hengyang rail center. The meaning was plain; unless the Japanese were stopped soon, Wuchow would be cut off from Free China.

Two weeks later Bill found his calculations were irrelevant; a Japanese drive out of Canton was moving directly up the West River toward Wuchow. The major Chinese elements had been thrown into the battle to the north, trying desperately to protect the American air bases threatened by the Japanese drive. The troops left to defend the drive coming from the east could only hope to slow the advance of the Japanese war machine. Being the only Baptist missionary left at Wuchow and completely responsible for the hospital and the total missionary effort thereabout, Bill knew he would have to decide "to be occupied" or to evacuate. He prayed for wisdom.

In Kweilin, Dr. Robert E. Beddoe, now acting field representative for the Foreign Mission Board, also realized the implications of the

81

Japanese drive. In typically decisive manner, he telegraphed the situation to Dr. M. Theron Rankin, who had succeeded Dr. Maddry as executive secretary, with the advice—"Evacuate all missionary personnel." On the 21st of June, Dr. Rankin cabled Beddoe to urge all missionaries to return to America on the first available transportation. Those who could not secure transportation were to move west immediately. Wallace was to evacuate Wuchow.

When Bill received Dr. Beddoe's instructions, he understood for the first time the crushing weight of responsibility that was his. Since the Japanese drive out of Canton had begun, Wuchow had been a veritable logjam of humanity, with refugees moving ahead of the Japanese offensive. The hospital was taxed to the very limits of its capabilities and all its members were working around the clock. Almost daily they were bombed by Japanese planes. The roar of their motors, the scream of falling bombs, the explosions and flames, and red and white tracers arching across the heavens were all a part of the daily scene.

To evacuate would mean to run out on the greatest challenge the hospital had ever faced. But to stay . . .? Bill had no stomach for Japanese occupation; he knew too much from the incident in Canton. Also, he could not risk the violation of the women of his staff and possible destruction of the valuable equipment that this bleeding land so desperately needed. If he tried to stay to the last possible moment, how would he get out? And how could he move that equipment? Calling the staff together, he explained the situation as he saw it, simply and unadorned. He did not try to hide the danger, but he was quick to point out their vital role. To his deep satisfaction, they agreed that the Stout Memorial Hospital could not leave the scene of the battle. They were willing to stay with him, even to the time of the coming of the Japanese themselves if Bill felt they could serve the purpose to which God had called them.

In a hurriedly scribbled note, totally devoid of heroic statements that more poetic men would have surely tried to make at such a time, he told Beddoe that they would stay for the time being.

Dr. Beddoe was frustrated by Wallace's action, but he knew his man. He telegraphed Dr. Rankin of the plans for the rest of the mission and then said, "I believe Dr. Wallace will stay until and if the enemy takes the city. I know nothing I can say or do will influence his opinion or actions in the slightest."

But Bill's problems were not all in terms of the inexhaustible tide of sick and wounded. Stout Memorial Hospital was without a director for nurses' training, one of its most fruitful ministries. A month before moving to Kweilin, Beddoe bombarded the Foreign Mission Board with demands for a missionary nurse. When Bill assumed responsibility for the hospital, he intensified the pleas for a nurse. Whenever he heard of a nurse having to leave another area because of war, he immediately wrote to her, often forgetting to send the Board a carbon. When he heard of a nurse in the States who was interested, he wrote directly to her, urging her to come with all possible haste.

Finally it seemed his persistency and prayers were to be rewarded. Missionary Nurse Lucy Wright, who had served for twenty years in the Shantung Province of North China until she had been driven out by the Japanese in 1940, volunteered to go to Wuchow. Though she was Mandarin-speaking, the Board knew her training and understanding of the Chinese would more than make up for this handicap. She would go to Wuchow.

Bill literally danced with joy when he heard that Lucy Wright had left the States for Wuchow. But he did not reckon with the frustrations of a global war. It took her eight long months on the proverbial "slow boat to China" to reach, not China, but India. Using all her feminine persuasion, she arranged to be flown over "The Hump" by a military plane to Kweichow. She could get no farther, and took up residence in an evacuated mission station with several other stranded missionaries. The Japanese advance had cut her off from Wuchow.

In the meantime, the American consul was doing everything but ordering Bill to close the hospital and come out. After receiving a final order, Bill called his staff together and put the matter once again to them. What should they do? Stay on! And the people of Wuchow took note. All the foreigners had gone from their city, but Waa Í Saang was still there, and the hospital was still open.

"There can be no real danger," they reassured one another, "as long as the Baptist hospital stays open."

In the fall of 1943 the governor of the Kwangsi Province, the Honorable H. Wong, was brought to the Stout Memorial Hospital more dead than alive with ruptured appendix. Dreaded peritonitis was in its advanced stages and it seemed little could be done. He had been treated by the government hospital until the doctors there, realizing that they could lose face with the death of such a high official, recommended that he be sent to Dr. Wallace. After a brilliant piece of surgery, Bill ordered a cot brought into the governor's room and he personally watched over him in a tenacious battle that saved the governor's life.

When the official recovered, he tried to make Bill accept expensive gifts. He even wanted to reward him in a formal Wuchow ceremony. But Bill resisted every move and pointed out very firmly to the governor that he was doing his job and that he already had his reward in seeing the governor get well. The governor did not forget the slender doctor.

In July the people of Wuchow, realizing that the inexorable Japanese advance would surely engulf them before too long, began to evacuate the city. The governor, hearing of the move, sent three large river barges and a motor launch to the docks of Wuchow with orders to evacuate Dr. Bill Wallace and the hospital staff. But Bill still refused to abandon the hospital. Then, the governor ordered his boats to wait for the doctor if they had to wait until the Japanese came. They were to let nothing drive them from their patient wait for their courageous cargo.

Bill now experienced a period of agonizing reappraisal. As he watched his staff work themselves to exhaustion and illness under the increasingly dangerous conditions—the bombers would not let them alone—he asked himself over and over again, "Am I doing the right thing?" Finally, taking a chance he could get one more cable out, he wired Dr. Rankin, asking advice. Rankin, sensitive to the struggle that was going on in the missionary's soul, replied, "We can't advise, but we can support you with prayers and confidence as you stay or leave."

The early days of September became more action-packed and tension-filled. The march of refugees was increasing. The city itself was badly wrecked by the continuing bombings. A large portion of the population was joining the pitiful stream of humanity to the west. Now the hospital was ministering to soldiers. Daily, they were brought in; by the 10th of September even that flow stopped. Then the soldiers were not coming to Wuchow; they were coming through Wuchow. It did not take a military strategist to know that the hunger-weakened, poorly-clothed, ridiculously-armed soldiery that was moving through was the remnant of a defeated army.

Still Bill waited, his staff blindly trusting in his judgment. He could not leave with a hospital full of patients. Hoping to reduce the number of patients in the hospital, he and his staff began to treat patients and move them out as soon as possible. By September 12, they were able to evacuate all but a few of the more seriously wounded.

On September 12, Bill received word from the city fathers that the city itself was to be evacuated. Now he made his decision. It was time to go. If they stayed, their task might be ended forever, but if they left, following the torn and suffering multitude west, they could continue to fulfil their ministry. On the night of September 12, Bill called his staff together and outlined his plan.

They would take every possible piece of equipment with them and load the barges. They would go west until they found a place that was safe and there they would find some kind of quarters to set up their hospital. They would continue to serve. The Stout Memorial Hospital would not die; it would move, but it would not die. The hospital was not the building any more than a church is a building. The hospital was the staff, and the spirit of service was in the name of the Lord Jesus Christ. They would move the hospital.

All of this Bill said simply, but the new hope, the dream that the missionary doctor had envisioned, thrilled his staff and they enthusiastically made the necessary preparations. It took four days to dismantle the equipment and complete the loading of the barges. The task was done primarily under the cover of night because Japanese fighter planes, harassing the retreating Nationalists, were a constant threat. Bill turned over the medical chores to his capable residents and gave himself completely to the supervision of the move. His fellow workers marveled at his ability to dismantle complicated machinery and reduce bulky items to compact kits that could be crated and loaded onto the large barges still patiently waiting at the Wuchow docks.

On the night of September 16, a final check was made at the hospital and then the staff walked down through the deserted streets, carrying what few belongings they themselves were taking. There were brief backward looks at the proud hospital building, battle-scarred, but still standing. It symbolized all they were doing, and it had come to mean to them what it had come to mean to the people, "the life of China."

As Bill walked through the streets of Wuchow, he was conscious of the havoc wrought there. Small fires, still burning from the day's raid, cast an eerie glow on the shadowy staff. At Bill's insistence, white uniforms had been packed and all were dressed in the black muslin that was summer dress for most Chinese. They would be easy enough targets on the river without their white clothing.

Bill and his staff boarded the barges, and the small gunboat that was to pull them to safety began to strain against the towlines, slowly moving its burden out into the broad West River that shimmered a peaceful paradox beneath the September moon. Their journey into the wilderness had begun.

Dawn the next day found the group well upriver from Wuchow, and they took cover at the edge of the river under sheltering bamboos. The next night's journey brought them to the mouth of a small river which led to a relatively obscure town, Yung-Yuen. Because Yung-Yuen was in such an out-of-the-way place, Bill thought it would be a safer place to go. It was bound to be filled with refugees. The main Japanese drives were aimed at more promising targets. Not knowing how long they would be safe on the river, Bill, after a moment of indecision, ordered the motor launch to pull into the tributary and head for Yung-Yuen.

Their progress up the river was little more than a painful creep. The current was much stronger than they had anticipated. On the second day, Japanese planes roared overhead. All the people had to abandon the barges and take cover in caves along the river's edge.

That evening as Bill was supervising the reloading of a barge, he heard someone call:

"Waa I Saang! Waa I Saang! Come here at once!"

He saw Dr. Wong calling him from a point up the trail that meandered alongside the river. Standing by him was a Chinese peasant loaded down with his few possessions.

"What is the matter, Dr. Wong?" Bill asked as he came near them.

"This man has just come from Yung-Yuen. He says the Japanese have taken the town and are moving down this river toward Tun-Yuen. He says they cannot be more than ten miles behind him."

"It is providential we stopped in these caves," Bill said. "Now let's get going." He ran down to the motor launch. In a few moments the loading was completed and they turned back toward Tun-Yuen and the West River.

They made much faster progress as they traveled with the aid of the current; but Bill had a new worry. Not only were the Japanese just ten miles behind them, but he was not sure that they were not directly ahead also. Earlier in the day he heard on his radio that Wuchow had fallen. No date was given, and he did not know how long after their departure it had occurred, but he knew the drive was moving steadily upriver. Japanese gunboats might be preceding them. But, he thought, as his eyes tried to pierce the darkness ahead, there is no other place to go. They would not stand a chance if they tried to take to the hills. Praying silently, he waited for the dawn.

Shortly after dawn they arrived at Tun-Yuen. They had made the return journey in a third of the time it had taken them to move upriver. And, to their great relief, the Japanese had not arrived.

Again they pulled out into the broad West River and continued a westerly course. The next town was Kwei-Peng, where again they faced a choice. They could go north toward Luichow, a strong military point which the Chinese and Americans together might hold. To the west was Nanning.

Calling his doctors together, Bill spread the map out before them

and outlined the possibilities. If they went to Luichow, they would
be able to go only so far by boat and then would have to find some
kind of land transportation. It would be much cheaper to go by
river to Nanning. However, the Japanese drive from Indochina was
moving in that direction and they had no way of knowing how much
progress it was making. But, as one of the doctors pointed out, neither did they have news as to how close the Japanese were to
Luichow. Bill made his decision. They would go to Nanning. At
least it would enable them to stay with their barges and prevent the
delay of unloading them or the tragedy of abandoning their equipment.

Still another problem confronted him. West from Kwei-Peng the
gunboat pulling the barges was to be pressed into the battle for this
area and could not go with them any farther. Taking a doctor with
him who knew Mandarin, Bill went into Kwei-Peng to find the
owners of the few launches in town and see if he could hire someone
to take them to Nanning. He did—after agreeing to pay an exorbi-
tant sum for the service. As incredible as it seemed, profiteers were
milking every possible profit out of the situation.

Food was more and more difficult to find. Except for the fast-
diminishing supplies they brought with them, Bill and his group
were dependent for their foodstuffs upon pitiful amounts of rice
purchased at fantastic prices.

The next few days were a long nightmare. First they came to
rapids which the launch did not have power to navigate. Bill organized his already weakened staff into crews to pull heavy towlines
to clear the rapids. They labored for hours at the exhausting task.
Finally, when all of them were once again on the barges, over half
the staff were sick with diarrhea and fever.

Like a watchful father, Bill made the rounds of patients on each
barge, dispensing carefully hoarded medicines and soothing fevered
brows, uttering brief words of encouragement. When he could do
no more, he threw down his mat in their midst and collapsed for a
few hours of desperately needed sleep.

Chinese had been accustomed to foreigners—even missionaries—
having separate quarters and eating different food. Colonialism had

given a cast to the white man's life in the Orient that made this the normal, even expected, thing. But Bill Wallace, the revered Waa I Saang, slept in their midst, accepted their common portion, turned aside food himself that they might have it. As one of them so aptly phrased it, "He actually lived before us the life of Christ."

The strange caravan was met by military authorities in Nanning, and Bill was told it would not be safe to stay there. He was advised to proceed to the little town of Poseh. The authorities felt the Japanese would be contained at Nanning, and if Bill and his group could reach Poseh, surely they could stop and begin their ministry.

But Bill's expensive transportation was gone. He was left with the clumsy, heavily loaded barges and no power to move on. Working through the day, Bill and the men of his staff, summoning all their ingenuity, rigged up clumsy, but fairly effective sails for each barge. Then, with towlines and long poles, they moved toward Poseh. When they were fortunate, the wind furnished enough power to keep them inching along. At other times, they poled along the shallows near the bank of the river. At still other times, they poled, pulled, and tried to sail in order to keep ahead of the inexorable march of death behind them.

Nearly night of the first day out of Nanning, Bill sat down on a box at the rear of the last barge with pencil and paper to get off a note to Dr. Rankin to let him know they had escaped. Bill had forgotten how many days they had been out, but he knew that friends and loved ones would be worried.

In the broad, characteristic scrawl of his medically trained hand, he wrote, "We left Wuchow on September 16 just ahead of the Japanese. 'We' includes our hospital equipment and staff and nurses, a total of fifty-five people. We had actually hoped to re-establish ourselves in Nanning, but we were told to move to Poseh in southern Kwangsi. It will probably take us ten days to get there if we get there at all.

"Moving expenses have been tremendous and now we are facing a hard winter, but we are doing our best to keep the Stout Memorial Hospital intact. It's the hope of every one of us that it not die. Our staff and nurses have been faithful to the hospital through it all.

It is our wish that someday, some happy day, we may return to Wuchow.

"I do not know if we can survive or not, but we're going to try. And if we fail, we will have the assurance that we failed trying.

"Be good." BILL WALLACE.

As he finished the letter, he was aware of Dr. Wong beside him. Together they watched the twilight give way to night. Since leaving Nanning, they had marked its location by a great pillar of smoke— the scorched earth policy. Now as night fell, the pillar of smoke glowed red with the fires that fed it.

The Chinese Christian said, "We are like the people of Israel in the wilderness. We have a pillar of cloud by day and a pillar of fire by night."

11

The Hospital in the Wilderness

The American transport plane banked sharply and began its descent through the thick clouds shielding its destination. Lucy Wright pressed her face against the window for the first glimpse of Poseh. She was sure the pilot had miscalculated and would fly right into the ground when the plane broke through the clouds and the south China countryside greeted her with verdant greens and rich browns. Directly ahead was a gray huddle of buildings and the Poseh airstrip, and, she desperately hoped, the refugee staff of the Stout Memorial Hospital.

She thanked the crew-cut Georgia boy who had flown her from the village where she had impatiently awaited the end of the Japanese offensive. Then she picked up her duffel bag and quick-stepped toward a bleak quonset hut she assumed was the terminal. There, to her dismay, she learned that a Chinese hospital group headed by an American missionary had already left.

"They stayed here a week," an American soldier told her. "Dr. Wallace operated a combined Chinese-American hospital, serving both the military and the citizens."

Lucy asked, "Did they go back to Nanning when it was retaken from the Japanese?"

"Yes," the soldier replied. "Dr. Wallace said it was time to begin to push back toward Wuchow. He thought victory was on its way. That's one of the hardest-working outfits I've ever seen," he added seriously. "And he helped me through a rough sickness."

The soldier told Lucy how Dr. Wallace had tenderly treated him for a case of hookworm. He also told her he was a Baptist from Dallas, Texas.

"Somehow, I've got to catch up with Dr. Wallace and his hospital group," Lucy said.

91

"You might hitch a ride with those trucks at the other end of the field, if you're lucky. They are going to Nanning, I hear," the soldier said.

Moments later, the determined nurse was in the cab of a truck loaded with relief supplies and was on her way to Nanning.

"Have you been to Nanning?" she asked the driver.

"Yes, ma'am; I'm stationed there. But if you haven't been there, I wouldn't want you to get your hopes up. It's not much town."

"Never mind that. Do you know where Dr. Wallace is located?"

"Dr. Wallace? I'm afraid not, ma'am. Nanning is crawling with people from all over China."

"Guess you would not have a chance to see him, at that." Lucy was genuinely disappointed. She was afraid they had moved again. She was ready to despair of ever reaching the group she had set out to help in the fall of 1943. It was now June, 1945.

"Wait a minute," the driver said. "Are you talking about a tall, thin American—a missionary with about fifty Chinese with him?"

"That's right—that's Bill Wallace." A smile as broad as all China spread across Lucy's tanned features.

"I can take you right by there. I didn't know his name, but everybody knows about him. That crowd is a legend in these parts. I hear they came from 'way down the West River—sailed right through the entire Japanese army. The Chinese think they're protected by angels or something."

"They're from Wuchow," she volunteered. "I have been trying to catch up with them for over a year."

"Well, hold on, ma'am, you're practically there!"

Moments later, Lucy, in dust-covered army fatigues, hurried to find Bill Wallace. When she identified herself, she touched off a joyous celebration. And, wonder of wonders, the reticent Dr. Wallace made a forty-five-minute speech.

The occasion was a staff meeting called to welcome the long-awaited nurse. To the Mandarin-speaking Lucy Wright, Bill's Tennessee-accented Cantonese was largely unintelligible, but she sensed what he was saying from the faces of his hearers.

As Bill talked in slow, now measured, now faltering words, Lucy

Wright realized that the little band had been forged into a close-knit Christian family by the hardships they had endured together. She felt the same pride in joining them that she thought a soldier must feel when he becomes a part of a proud and honored military unit. She found herself envying them the experiences that mediated such cohesive power.

"And we will return soon." She could tell he was talking of the future now and leading them with him. "We will return to Wuchow and we will rebuild and this old hospital will keep right on with an unbroken history. I believe God has spared us for this task."

It was not an eloquent speech, but Lucy Wright wished she could take it down word for word. She was sure that the heart of Bill Wallace was more open in this moment than ever before.

Days later she heard the story of their adventures from one of the English-speaking nurses with whom she was rooming. She had known of their trek to Poseh, but from there she had only pieces of the story.

"Where in the world did you stay in Poseh?" Lucy asked. "I was there this morning and it doesn't look like much."

"It wasn't much," the Chinese nurse answered. "Dr. Wallace went to the authorities, told them that we were a hospital group and would like to set up and serve the people there. The town elders said we could use an old Confucian temple and an abandoned school building. Actually, it was Governor Wong of Kwangsi who made this possible, the same man who made available the boat for us. We were overwhelmed by this generous act until we realized that they let us have the temple because no one else would use it. The townspeople said it was inhabited by devils. After we moved in, we became local heroes because the people figured Dr. Wallace purged the place of the demons who were possessing it."

Lucy laughed, "The medical association would appreciate Dr. Wallace's abilities as an exorcist."

"Well, I don't know about that; but under his leadership we soon transformed that filthy place into a hospital. You've never seen so many makeshift odds and ends in your life. Dr. Wallace was positively ingenious, bringing in electric power, setting up a water and

sewage system, helping us to erect bamboo curtains and secure mats
for beds—even obtaining a chemical which he mixed to restore our
uniforms to their original whiteness. He always wanted us looking
like a hospital, as well as acting like one."

Lucy was silent. The nurse continued, caught up in her narrative.
"Poseh was an epidemic area of a malignant malaria. Also, cholera
and other diseases were rampant, and it seemed three quarters of
the population was sick. We were no exception. Nearly half our
staff was down with malaria; and, of course, being weakened by
poor food and the rigors of our trip, we were easy prey for whatever was circulating. One of the nurses developed a severe malaria
psychosis. Have you ever seen one of those?"

Lucy nodded, remembering the horror of patients screaming in
the night, totally out of their minds with the ravages of the fever.

"You should have seen Dr. Wallace with her. She was like an
animal and it was as if he had some kind of magic charm. When
nobody else was able to do anything with her, he quieted her. He
stayed by her bedside for forty-eight hours until he was sure she
was through the crisis.

"Up to this time, we had lost no one, but I am sorry to say that
ended at Poseh. You see, we heard that the Japanese were threatening Poseh. We thought we were safe, but American planes spotted
a column of Japanese who had by-passed Nanning and were only
twenty miles from us. We were heartsick. I think in the shape we
were in, we were ready to stay there and take whatever came. However, Dr. Wallace got us to our feet again, and somehow we re-
packed our equipment. As we were trying to figure out how to get
it back to the boats, he drove up with an ambulance that he had
found someplace. To this day, I don't know where he got it.

"When the ambulance was about to complete hauling our equipment to the boats, we discovered that one of our doctors, Dr. Chow
Kwan Pok, was desperately ill. Dr. Wallace was treating him for
ulcers, but, without the proper diet, he suffered a severe relapse. He
hemorrhaged right at the time we should have been leaving. We
could hear guns in the distance.

"Dr. Wallace would not hear of moving him. We sat there while he did everything he could for Dr. Pok, but in that place there was so little we could do. I'll never forget that night. We were not allowed to have any light because the Japanese planes had bombed Poseh several times. Silently, we sat around the building watching Dr. Wallace bend over his patient. Not many of us slept that night. The guns were coming closer and closer. Just before dawn, Dr. Wallace urged us all to get on the boat and go, but then it was our turn to be insistent. We refused, but I think he was grateful for it.

"Dr. Pok died shortly after dawn, despite all Dr. Wallace could do. I never want to be in a situation like that again. We were actually praying that he would either recover enough to travel or go ahead and die. I know it sounds terrible, but you cannot imagine the anxiety of hearing those guns coming closer and measuring them with the labored breath of a life hanging in balance."

Lucy could imagine the drama of the moment, but she knew that was nothing to the actual experience.

"This was the only time I came close to getting impatient with Waa I Saang. He was adamant at the point of securing a coffin and giving Dr. Pok a Christian burial. All the stores were closed and barred, as most of the townspeople had fled. Dr. Wallace and the evangelist finally located a funeral-shop owner who had not left. Waa I Saang bought a coffin from him, but the man would not help him transport it back where we were. Dr. Wallace had to take it apart and we carried it piece by piece to a small hill back of the old temple. There Dr. Wallace put the coffin back together and then he carried the body of Dr. Chow up the hill, where we held the funeral.

"Now the guns, nearer than ever, were being rivaled by thunder from the heavens. Just before we began the service, it started to rain. Someone said, 'Heaven cries with us on this day.' Dr. Wallace read some Scripture passages from his little pocket Testament and led a prayer. Then each of us picked up some of the dirt which was now almost mud and tossed it in. As soon as the grave was filled, we ran down the hill to the river and boarded the boats."

The Oriental nurse's cheeks were wet now and she paused for a moment, daubing at her face with a small handkerchief.

"That may have been our saddest moment, but it certainly wasn't our most difficult. Poling and pulling the boats, we moved on down to a little village called Fok-Luk. The conditions there were horrible. Refugees were everywhere. Bodies were lying in the streets; there was no one to move them. We had to avoid wild pigs who were preying on the dead. They were so famished they sometimes assaulted the living. People were too weak even to catch them.

"A Japanese army had moved up from Indochina to the south and was trying to join the army that had taken Nanning. We were trapped in the middle. We camped outside Fok-Luk and daily ran to the nearby caves to take refuge from the Japanese dive bombers. Those caves were sweltering masses of stinking flesh. I still remember their stench. And the fear. You could smell the fear.

"This was the time I think we were in most danger. Many of us were ready to move off on our own and find food where we could, but Dr. Wallace kept us together. He encouraged us, led us in prayer, rationed the food, and went out daily to find more.

"It was while at Fok-Luk that I saw Dr. Wallace refuse his rice allowance and give it to a nurse who was desperately ill with fever. Most of us were sick with diarrhea or fever. Later on I saw him behind the cook tent we had rigged up. He was eating grains of burned rice, hardly palatable, that had been thrown away. When he realized I had seen him, he was terribly embarrassed.

"No, he wasn't ashamed of eating that food; no one else would have had it, as hungry as we were. I think he was embarrassed because he did not want me to know how hungry he was.

"He was so thin I thought he would blow away if a good wind came along. Somehow, however, he stayed well. He showed us how to eat the bones of what few fowl we found, to get needed vitamins. I believe his unorthodox methods saved all our lives during this period. He was so good, watching over each of us, cheering us, caring for the sick, and doing everything he could to provide for our comfort.

"I don't want to offend you, Miss Wright, but we Chinese are not used to seeing Americans or Europeans do things like this. We know the missionaries love us, but there was always a difference.

They lived their way and we lived ours, but Dr. Wallace didn't know about the difference. He was one of us; he accepted our portion—all of it."

"I can see why you all love him as you do," Lucy said. "How long were you there before you returned to Poseh?"

"I am afraid we weren't thinking about returning then. The Japanese killed several soldiers right outside Fok-Luk about a week after we arrived, and we fled for our lives during the night. We left our equipment where it was. Fortunately, we were able to recover it later.

"This time we moved by foot to a little village called Tung-Ling. This was the time I felt most sorry for Dr. Wallace. In pulling the boat along the banks of the river out of Nanning, he had worn out his one pair of shoes, a ragged pair of tennis shoes. Now he was walking through the paper he had stuffed in the bottom of them.

"He fell down by the side of the road the second day and we all feared he had had a heart attack or something. An American soldier had given us two horses the day before, and we put him up on one and kept going. When he recovered sufficiently to realize what was happening, he immediately insisted upon getting off and putting one of the nurses on. I don't know how we lived during those days. We just existed at Tung-Ling. It was a wonderful day when a column of American soldiers came through and told us that Poseh had been retaken."

"And you were all still together?" Lucy asked.

"All together." The nurse smiled. "And you have never seen a more grateful group. Daily we prayed. We must have sounded like what you Americans call 'holy rollers.' I am afraid our prayers were loud and our tears many, but daily we sought God.

"That was the only time we broke up for a while. Dr. Wallace found transportation for us a few at a time with American trucks that were coming through. The soldiers seemed so surprised to see him way out there and it cheered us to observe him laughing and talking with people from back home.

"When we all got back to Poseh, he came in a few days later with our equipment from the place where he had abandoned it.

That's when we began our hospital. I think the hospital was Dr. Wallace's idea, I mean to join together with the other medical people, including the military, and establish the 'Chinese-American Combined Hospital.' "

Lucy said, "You must have been treating a lot of American soldiers. I met one back in Poseh who had been in your hospital with hookworm."

"Yes, we treated the ulcer-ridden, also soldiers infected with hookworm, dysentery, nutritional diarrhea, malaria, relapsing fever—all of it. After one particularly hard battle with a pocket of Japanese nearby, we treated the wounded. But we also lost one of our nurses at that time. We never did know exactly what she died of, but it was like losing a sister. Dr. Wallace mourned her as a daughter." Nurse Luk stopped and smiled. "And by God's grace, we've been here ever since."

"Yes," Lucy said, "by God's grace."

The next day, after Bill Wallace introduced her to the hospital routine, Lucy made calls with him. She marveled at his rapport with both the Chinese and American soldiers that were being treated there. She noted a unique sense of humor and a remarkable facility for getting people to talk about themselves and their interests. It was an effective form of therapy.

The hospital was a 150-bed unit, if you can call strung rope and straw mats hospital beds. Late that day, however, as she assisted him in surgery, she realized that this hospital had nothing for which to apologize, even in such primitive conditions.

The hospital in the wilderness served through the summer in Nanning. With August 14, came V-J Day. The Japanese emperor had surrendered unconditionally, and his armies were leaving China.

The hospital group could hardly believe it. They were going home! All day long the hospital became the scene for spontaneous celebrations. Lucy saw grateful American soldiers come bringing food and other gifts, and the crisp discipline of the wards dissolve into a milieu of joy. The center of attention, despite all his effort to fade into the background, was the grinning doctor who had faithfully fulfilled the role of Moses during these days in the wilderness.

The next day the military staged a formal celebration and the Stout Memorial nurses were asked to sing. Their voices rang out in crystal clarity with joy and gratitude. That evening, at a party sponsored by the Americans, they were asked to sing again. Like many celebrations in those exuberant days, the party had become extremely wild, with a lot of drinking and hilarity. Lucy Wright and the other nurses, used to singing hymns, were at a loss at what to do. They turned to Bill, seeking advice. He grinned and said, "Get up there and sing a hymn." They did and they were again marvelously received.

It seems their hymn touched the hearts of the better side of the celebrants and turned their thoughts from unrestrained gaiety to memories of home, to the faith of their fathers, and gratitude to an almighty God. It was a fitting climax to the ministry of the hospital in the wilderness.

The same God that provided for their exodus now provided for their return to Wuchow. Grateful American officials, many of whom had experienced the ministry of the "refugeeing hospital" firsthand, threw themselves enthusiastically into the project of returning the hospital staff. A large flatboat was found for a ridiculously low price and Bill wondered what kind of coercion had taken place. Shortly, a motor launch was provided to tow them. Then, American soldiers attached to the units Dr. Wallace and his staff had served, built an ingenious kitchen-boat that could be towed along behind the barge which would carry the staff and its equipment.

On a sparkling September morning, they began the last leg of their strange odyssey. The docks of Nanning were lined with grateful citizens and cheering soldiers. As the staff waved to their crisis-born friends, the broad West River moved them along, and soon Nanning faded into the distance. They were on their way home.

It was a four-day trip, but a trip in sharp contrast with the painful flight that had taken place nearly a year earlier. It was a time of rest and singing and individual meditation. Lucy noticed that Bill sat on the sidelines most of the journey, aware of the exhaustion that comes from a total experience.

All afternoon of the last day of the trip, the staff laughed and called out to one another as familiar scenes appeared on the horizon. As they gathered for their evening meal around the charcoal braziers that kept their food warm, they decided to sing hymns into Wuchow. Then the lights of Wuchow came into view, and they beheld the familiar skyline and hills basking under the benevolent stars that had witnessed their leave-taking. Rising to their feet, they voiced their joy in song.

> Crown Him with many crowns,
> The Lamb upon His throne;
> Hark! how the heavenly anthem drowns
> All music but its own:
> Awake, my soul, and sing
> Of Him who died for thee;
> And hail Him as thy matchless King
> Through all eternity.

Lucy Wright looked up as the smiling doctor approached with a letter in his hand. He said, "I have just written my sister, and I thought you might like to read the letter."

She took it and read it by firelight. Never had so much been said with so little.

DEAR SIS:

Wuchow.

Love,

BILL

12

Return to Wuchow and Home

The hospital building still stood, strong and stoic, but the interior and grounds were in shambles. The terrible destruction, along with the cholera which was decimating the town, quite depressed the returning staff. Only the wide grins of the welcoming populace cheered them.

Bill led his fellow physicians on a survey of the once-immaculate institution. The plumbing was clogged with brick and filth—the Japanese soldiers had stabled horses on the lower floor. There was no water, power, screens, or doors. The furniture was destroyed or gone. Vital pieces of hard-to-replace equipment were strewn over the grounds. A section of the roof was gone.

After the survey, he gathered the staff together at the steps. They were a tattered and tired lot and their forlorn faces reflected the almost impossible task they faced. Bill stood quietly looking over the group for a moment and then grinned. "We had better get with it. There are some sick people around here, and they need a hospital."

With that he turned and started up the steps. One by one they followed him. Shortly, they were enthusiastically engaged in reclaiming the beloved old building. There was a job to be done.

They recovered and cleaned salvaged equipment; they screened, scrubbed, and painted the first floor and, miraculously, had it looking reasonably antiseptic within a matter of days. Bill rigged up an ingenious still to manufacture intravenous saline for the treatment of cholera. He set up a crude but effective laboratory. With a borrowed acetylene torch, he converted some Japanese gasoline drums into a large storage tank for the water they boiled day and night. Drawing upon the mechanical skill that had characterized his youth, he built a hand-powered electric generator to furnish power and light for surgery. In one of the more dramatic moments, he cleared the building and defused three unexploded Japanese bombs.

Daily, he encouraged his staff toward the goal of receiving their first patient at the earliest possible moment, and they responded by working to the limit of their endurance. Just one week later, a proud and grateful group of doctors and nurses gathered in the bomb-scarred fifth-floor chapel to dedicate themselves to the task. Then they went downstairs and threw open the wrought iron gates. The Stout Memorial Hospital was open again!

Bill himself carried very little medical responsibility for the first few weeks, preferring instead to direct the rebuilding. He rebuilt the kitchen, personally constructing the brick oven they were to use for over a year. Since no construction men were available, he hired laborers and supervised the repair of the roof section that had been blasted away. This was his first failure; it fell in a week. Surveying the wreckage, he said, "Well, you can't win them all," and started over.

The staff were concerned about Bill's constant work with never a moment's relaxation. Lucy Wright accused Bill of being a Spartan. "I'll declare," she said, "he takes absolutely no thought for himself. He sleeps on a bamboo mat with a smooth log for a pillow. We procured two or three old beds, but he gave me one and sent the others to the nurses' quarters. He said he had been refugeeing so long he couldn't sleep on a bed.

"One day I managed to purchase some buffalo milk, oatmeal, and Indian butter and prepared him a meal. The way he carried on, you would have thought it was an embassy dinner.

"He has a childlike enthusiasm for the little things in life, and it is catching. One night he hollered for us to come to the door and we came running, expecting some kind of emergency. Instead, he wanted us to see our first full moon since returning to Wuchow."

Two months after their return, Bill heard of an outbreak of typhus fever in the Wuchow jail. It was a pitiful place, crowded to overflowing with political prisoners, as well as common criminals. He went to the city fathers and persuaded them that it was a health menace to the whole city (they would have cared very little for the welfare of the prisoners themselves). He gained permission to let his staff undertake to stamp out the typhus.

Daily, he took a contingent of volunteers and made the rounds of the filth-ridden cells and their disease-wasted inmates. Even the most distrustful and hardened of the prisoners soon came to regard him as an angel of mercy. He threatened and even bribed those in charge to make some sorely needed improvements and surprised all who knew him with the vigor and passion with which he tackled the project.

By Christmas Bill had the hospital back on a teaching level with a new class of nurses and two new interns. Returning from a trip to a nearby village one day, he unshouldered a sack of bleached bones—the remains of some poor peasant who had perished from unknown causes along the trail. Soon he had a perfect skeletoh erected and instructed his nurses in basic bone structure.

The next spring he received the glad news that Dr. Robert Beddoe was on his way back to China and the Stout Memorial Hospital. As soon as he arrived, Bill would take his second furlough, a time he anticipated with tremendous excitement. He needed some more study and, of course, he longed to see his sister and her family. And there was someone else he wanted to see—if she were still available.

Lucy helped the latter desire grow. With a twinkle in her eye, she often quoted "the girl's" letters to the more-than-just-a-little-interested doctor. Bill knew that Lucy carried on a lively correspondence with the young lady he had become fond of on his first furlough.

Then the Beddoes arrived, and after a short but poignant reunion, Bill was gone, homeward bound. Soon he was in Richmond, Virginia. He called his friend for a date as casually as if he had seen her the week before, instead of five long years. He did not know that Lucy Wright had written her recently:

". . . By the time you read this letter, our mutual friend will be on the high seas returning to America. I have a feeling you will hear from him, and soon. Also I have a feeling that he will tell you very little about these past few years, and that is a shame. He has a heroic and unbelievable story to share. But maybe he will tell you; as I always say, never underestimate the power of a woman. . . ."

Richmond's Jefferson Hotel has long been famous for its old Southern charm. Crystal, candlelight, gracious service, and excellent food are its hallmark. It was Bill's favorite place to take this friend. As she sat across the exquisitely set table from him, she smiled at the contrast it must afford to the scenes he had so recently left.

"What are you smiling about?" Bill was thoroughly enjoying himself. War, disease, death, and famine were forgotten. He was with a friend he had sorely missed and he was relaxed and content.

"I was just thinking that this must seem almost unreal after what you have just been through."

"That's funny, I was just thinking how unreal all of that seemed in light of this. I guess I am a man who lives only in the present."

"But you live the present so well." It slipped out before she realized it, and she was embarrassed. She hurriedly continued. "I do wish you would not be so reticent in sharing your experiences, though. They could mean so much to the men and women who have prayed for you and supported you, not to mention the young people who would really be challenged by them." Now she seemed to be scolding and she added, "I guess I sound rather petulant."

He smiled. "That's all right; it's true." Bill slowly turned the crystal water glass before him, thinking back now. "I really do have a story to tell, but I don't know how to tell it. Where would I begin? I would have to tell the story of fifty different people who are as much a part of it as I am and whose lives were my inspiration. I would have to tell of the hundreds I met along the way, of a wonderful Chinese doctor buried in a chilling Kwangsi rain, of fuzzy-faced American soldiers and wrinkled peasants. But most of all, my difficulty now is that 'the story' is behind me. I have a hard time living anything over again."

They both fell silent as a waiter cleared the dishes and poured fresh coffee. Then she began to ask questions. Having been born in China, she was familiar with many of the people and places where Bill labored, and there was much she wanted to hear. But as he

talked, she felt that he was leading up to something else—waiting
for an opportunity to introduce it. On the way to the hotel he had
shown her a set of application forms for missionary service he had
picked up at the Board . . . "in case I find someone interested in
going to China." Was she mistaken or had he said it pointedly as
if she might be that one?

She was hardly listening to him now. Though she was fully committed to Christian service and had been reared in a missionary
family, she had never experienced that personal call she felt was so
necessary for the missionary task. It had occurred to her that God
might call her through a husband, and if he did, she would go. Did
Bill want her to go with him when he returned? Was he waiting
for her to say that God had called her? For just a moment she felt
he was poignantly reaching out for her to say just that.

Both of them sensed the razor-edge of the moment. It under-
mined the surface conversation all through the magic evening. But
her feelings lacked that kind of assurance, and she felt intuitively
that his did, too.

The subject never emerged. The decision was made in unspoken
dimensions. Before they parted, they seemed to know that, though
their friendship would be something both of them would cherish
until the end of their days, they were meant to go their separate
ways. The unseen Planner of such things seemed to will other des-
tinies for them.

In keeping with his abiding passion, Bill Wallace had planned
this second furlough to better prepare himself to practice "the best
medicine." Great strides had been taken in surgical and medical
techniques during the war years, and he wanted to master what
he could before returning to his task. It was a time to "sharpen his
tools." As he had often lectured the resident physicians who worked
beside him in China, "The physician's education is an ever-continu-
ing one. A doctor cannot rest on his laurels."

His first tour was at Chicago's famous Cook County School of
Medicine. He enrolled in three consecutive courses: roentgenology,
general surgery, and thoracic surgery. From October to January,
he labored in the medical center with a seemingly insatiable appe-

tite to learn. Beyond the lectures and specific assignments, he haunted the medical library, devouring journals and reading night after night to master the breakthroughs in research. He was a constant spectator in the operating theatre, and more than one well-known surgeon found himself being interrogated in chance meetings by the inquisitive missionary doctor.

When he finished his courses in Chicago, he made a brief trip to Knoxville for a few cherished moments with the Stegalls. Then he journeyed to New Orleans for a spring course in tropical medicines at Tulane University.

From a career standpoint, further studies in surgery would have been far more profitable. Instead, he chose to work in an area which would more suitably equip him to serve his beloved Chinese. Career and reputation did not prejudice his decisions.

In his rare moments of free time in New Orleans, Bill attended lectures at a nearby cancer clinic. In China he had noted the predominance of skin cancer among the people of a particular area served by the Stout Memorial Hospital. Notes and observations made in all these efforts were carefully recorded to be passed on in lectures to members of his own staff and the local medical association in Wuchow.

With spring's gentle appearance, his thought once again turned to China. Dr. Beddoe wrote that he was urgently needed. The old administrator was due retirement and was fully aware he could no longer carry the burden he had so ably borne so long. The people awaited Waa I Saang.

In April, Dr. Rankin visited Bill at New Orleans and later wrote Beddoe: "Bill seems to have just one single idea in mind: to get back to Wuchow on the first available passage after he completes his work in New Orleans." And as a pointed afterthought, Rankin added the answer to the unspoken question of those who looked for Wallace's return. "He seems to have no plans for taking anyone back with him."

His friend? Love came from another quarter. She was now engaged to an outstanding pastor.

Bill Wallace was excited about the prospects for his work. Rankin had brought wonderful news. Another doctor was being appointed and would sail soon for language school. Also, a wonderfully trained and experienced nurse had been appointed to serve at Wuchow. A dedicated young evangelist and his family were already in language school, and Rankin informed Bill that they, too, would be sent to Wuchow. A new day seemed to be dawning for the work to which he had given his life. His hopes soared.

Early in May, he completed his work in New Orleans and returned to Knoxville to complete arrangements for his return to China. Two days before he was to leave for San Francisco, he received a call from Dr. Herbert Acuff, a lifelong friend.

"William, I have some good news for you. You have been elected as a fellow in the International College of Surgeons."

Bill was stunned. He was aware that Dr. Peters had kept file on some of his more interesting cases in China, and early in the year he had given his old friend a full account of his medical findings during his twelve years in China. But he did not realize why the doctor was so interested in having the records, photos, and other papers. The International College of Surgeons! He thought he gave that up the day he turned down Dr. Peters' offer to join him.

"I don't know what to say, Dr. Acuff. I would not have thought that I qualified."

"You qualify, William. Perhaps in a way that few others have. You have done surgery of a nature and on a scale that makes many of us seem inexperienced by comparison. You deserve it, and I'm honored to be the one to inform you."

Bill Wallace had given up the thought of fame and prestige to plant his life in the strange environs of the Orient. But even from the shadows of the public eye, his light was too bright to ignore. His profession had recognized him and was proud of him.

It made him all the more eager to return to the task that was uniquely his, to which God called him, and in which God sustained him. He was humbly aware that any sacrifice he had ever imagined himself making had been abundantly matched by the blessings that came into his life as a result of his choice. It was hard to feel noble, he decided, when you were so busy feeling grateful.

Characteristically, his colleagues in Wuchow discovered his honor quite by accident. Bill never mentioned it.

The Stegalls tried their best to be cheerful as they drove Bill to the airport in Knoxville. He had gained twenty-two pounds during the year and looked in the pink of health. In fact, his sister decided he never looked better. But that did not relieve the haunting sadness she felt at their impending farewell. Bill sensed it, but so intent was he on his return to his work, that he did not respond.

Sydney Stegall said, "Take care of yourself, William, and drop us a line from time to time." Bill's brother-in-law, a Knoxville businessman, served as Bill's private business manager and purchasing agent. He considered it part of his Christian stewardship, and he loved Bill as his own flesh and blood. "Even if it's only an order for a set of test tubes, it reassures us about your well-being."

Bill looked at Sydney fondly and then at his sister, Ruth Lynn, and their son, Sandy. The youngster was trying manfully to hold back the tears threatening to overflow.

"Chief, I don't have a worry in the world. You will take care of Sis and Sandy, and I'll take care of me. The Lord will watch over us all."

13

The Eye of the Storm

Despite an uncertain political situation in China, Bill Wallace was encouraged as he began his third term of missionary service there. Dr. Sam Rankin and his wife, Miriam, were in language school in Canton along with Nurse Everley Hayes and a prince of a preacher, Ed Galloway, and his family. In less than a year they would be on the field in Wuchow.

The promise of new faces reminded Bill of the absence of older ones. Rex Ray was working at the leper colony, Tai Kam, and Bill missed the indomitable old evangelist. The Beddoes retired soon after Bill's return to China. He did not realize until they were gone how much he loved the veteran physician who was so much his opposite. The hospital was now officially in Bill's hands; always before it had been a temporary assignment. He felt the burden keenly, but the hospital was prospering. His 1947 report was a study of succinctness and depth.

"Every effort has been put forth to fulfil the mission of this hospital. The blind receive their sight and the halt and lame walk; the lepers are cleansed; the deaf hear and the poor have the gospel preached to them. It is our hope and prayer that the medical service in this institution shall be on that high plane befitting the glorious gospel which is preached daily within its walls."

Another face was there only briefly. Lucy Wright, who served so well during the latter days of the hospital in the wilderness and the period of rebuilding, was at the point of death when Bill returned from his furlough. Dr. Beddoe had diagnosed a ruptured ulcer, but neither he nor the Chinese physicians felt competent to perform the surgery indicated. Bill devoted himself incessantly to her case.

An operation did seem necessary, but it was extremely dangerous and Bill wanted to be sure it was the only chance. Ordering a steady flow of plasma and glucose, he decided to wait out her progress a little longer. Again and again he whispered reassuringly, "You are going to make it, Lucy. Stay in there. You are going to lick it."

Then he prayed. Several times he called others to join him in prayer at the nurse's bedside.

Bill Wallace believed deeply in the power of prayer. He often read and quoted James 5:14-15 to his resident doctors and nurses. "Is any sick among you? Let him call for the elders of the church; and let them pray over him, anointing him with oil in the name of the Lord. And the prayer of faith shall save the sick, and the Lord shall raise him up; and if he have committed sins, they shall be forgiven him."

He counted medical skills and drugs as God-given resources, but never as the only resources when sickness came. Too many of his cases had inexplicably responded in the face of what seemed inevitable death, for him not to believe firmly in that power just beyond man's exploring fingertips, available only through faith.

The tide turned and Lucy Wright, without surgery, began a slow but steady recovery. Bill appeared in her room one day with a heavy medical book. He opened it, showed her a marked section and then said, "God's done his part; let's do ours. Here is your problem." Then he turned the page. "Here is your cure."

Laying the volume on her nightstand, he stood up and smiled. "Now, don't dawdle."

Lucy recovered, but furlough time and a long convalescence were ahead. She left for the States after a tearful farewell.

Only Jessie Green, the able woman evangelist, remained of the prewar missionary staff with whom Bill had served.

Bill Wallace pondered the changing scene. It hardly seemed possible that he was now "the old China hand" at the station. And yet, he reminded himself, he, too, had changed. He was older, his hair thinner, but his hand was steady and he was more sure of himself. He was grateful for the experiences of the past and he was grateful for the opportunities of the present. If the relative tranquility of these days turned out to be only the eye of the storm, he was still ready to work while it was day.

In the summer of 1948, Wuchow was besieged by an epidemic of paratyphoid. Bill ordered each staff member to be inoculated and later went to secure serum for himself. The serum was a new typhoid-paratyphoid combination, and it was stored alongside the older typhoid serum which it replaced. Somehow Bill got the older serum, and later was ravaged by the dreaded paratyphoid.

His Chinese colleagues worked over him desperately. At first he was able to direct the treatment, then gradually delirium claimed him.

He was a boy again, ill with typhoid. He could make out the features of his beloved father hovering over him, tenderly ministering to him. He cried out, "Paps, I'm burning up!"

Nurse Luk wiped his brow and tried to calm him. At times, he was rational. "Get Newbern." He lifted himself up on one arm. Again he gasped, "Tell Newbern I must see him."

William Newbern, resident missionary at the nearby Christian and Missionary Alliance station, was one of Bill's closest friends. They had spent many hours together, and when he heard of Bill's illness, he rushed to his bedside.

Reaching up, Bill pulled him closer. "Tell the others to leave; I must make a confession."

Newbern gripped the clutching fingers of his friend. "I'm going to stay right here, Bill. You are going to be all right."

"Please," his voice was weak, but urgent, "please, Newbern, hear my confession."

Tears glistened on the preacher's cheeks. Who was he to hear this man's confession? Better he confess to Bill, fever and all. But at Bill's insistence, he sent the others out. When he returned to his side, Bill had lapsed back into his delirium. Patiently, Newbern waited. In a moment, the suffering doctor opened his eyes again.

"I've wronged my Lord, Newbern; I've neglected him terribly." Falling back, he groaned in the agony of his introspection while his friend listened quietly.

"I've been more concerned with the material prosperity of the hospital than I have with knowing my Lord. I've been too busy for him." He tried to rise. "Pray for me, Newbern; pray for me."

William Newbern was so choked up he could hardly speak. The exposed heart of the physician was so childishly simple; his faith was so uncomplicated. But he prayed.

In a moment, Bill gasped, "God is sufficient." He could trust his Lord. However, the disease continued to waste him and he grew steadily weaker.

The dawn of the next day brought light into the room again, but not hope. Bill's fever-wracked body twisted about; his dry, cracked lips shaped meaningless sounds. Growing concern furrowed the brow of Dr. Wong Taai Ning as he finished the pulse count. How many times had he taken the count since Waa I Saang took sick? He made quick notations on the chart and then, stretching, walked to the window. It had been a long night. Cushioning his head against his arm, he looked out over the city of Wuchow to the placid West River. Morning fogs were playing lazily above the mirrored surface. The tranquility of the old South China river mocked the turmoil in his own heart. He turned to look again at the wasted frame of his beloved colleague.

Movement below the window drew his attention to a silent, waiting crowd. Had they been there all night—this strangely mixed group of coolies and merchants, beggars and magistrates? As he watched, Nurse Luk walked from the building and began talking to someone among the waiting people. She gestured, shaking her head slowly. The low moan that moved among the assembled throng reminded Wong how much, how very much his people loved Dr. Bill Wallace.

He turned as the door opened and greeted Dr. Leung, a resident surgeon.

"How is Waa I Saang?"

"He is weak."

"Ai, the fever has made him thin."

"Yes. He is very thin, but he was never with much flesh."

"No, he ran up and down the stairs continually. He always worked too hard."

They were silent.

"Is there nothing else we can do?"

"Paratyphoid is especially hard on foreigners. His pulse is weaker; I really fear for him.

"Ai."

Dr. Wong, aware that someone had joined them, turned and solemnly greeted Miss Jessie Green. Afraid to look at her gravely-ill fellow missionary, her eyes sought Wong's for an encouraging word. Helpless, he simply looked back to the thin, almost aquiline features of the missionary surgeon.

With sudden determination, Jessie Green said, "I am going to wire the new doctors at Canton. Would you mind?"

"Oh, no, Goo-Goo Neung. But I fear, even if they come it will be only to share our grief."

"Nevertheless, I will wire them."

She hurried down the stairs and worked her way through the crowd at the door. A girl tugged at her sleeve. The little Oriental face beseeched her, the scar of an operation for harelip barely visible.

"Will Waa I Saang die?"

"We hope not, little one. You pray to the Lord Jesus to make him well."

"Yes, Goo-Goo Neung, I will do that."

Jessie Green's telegram reached Sam Rankin during the South China Mission meeting. It was hard for him to think of Bill Wallace near death. For several years he had heard of the magnificent ministry of the modest Tennessean. He yearned to work by his side, to catch his spirit, to learn from him, to watch the amazing ambidextrousness of his surgery. Was he to be denied this? By afternoon, he was on the West River steamer for Wuchow, and the next day he stood anxiously on the boat as Wuchow came into sight. Beside him stood Dr. Don Moore, who had volunteered to accompany him, and Nurse Everley Hayes. Impatiently, they watched the muddy waters churn as the West River steamer maneuvered alongside the Wuchow landing. Then Rankin spied Jessie Green on the dock.

"Here, Jessie! How is Bill?"

Her drawn look gave him a moment of panic. Were they too late?

"Thank God, you are here. There has been no change, but please come now. This boy will bring your things."

In the highly musical tones of Cantonese, she gave directions to the dutiful boy, then turned and hurriedly led them through the crowded streets toward the hospital compound.

By the following day the doctors had done all they could do. Their efforts seemed pitifully inadequate. There was really very little one could do; Sam reassured the distraught staff doctors at this point. Perhaps the liquids slowly dripping into his veins would make up for the alarming dehydration, but would they help in time? It was too early to tell if the blood transfusion (Everley's blood had been used) would help. They were grasping at straws. By all odds, Dr. Wallace should be dead. There was nothing to do but wait.

In the compound yard below, Everley Hayes and Jessie Green felt the same helplessness. The crowd outside the clinic walls—even larger now—still waited, suffering silently, patiently, in Oriental empathy. A few minutes previously Jessie had stepped to the gate to assure them Waa I Saang was still alive. All that could be done had been done. They could only pray—and wait. They prayed on "the Hill," led by Newbern. They prayed at the convent outside Wuchow, led by the priests who counted Bill Wallace a brother and an angel of mercy.

Everley suddenly realized she was extremely tired; the transfusion had weakened her. God grant that her blood would help! The hours since her arrival had passed very slowly. She sat down on a step, wearily. The Oriental knew how to wait; she would learn.

Late the next day, Sam Rankin, who had dozed off in a chair by Bill's bed, awoke with a start. For a minute he watched the quietly efficient ministries of Miss Lam, the surgical nurse; her concern was well contained, but he felt it.

Suddenly, she turned to him. "Is he not cooler?"

Quickly, Rankin rose and felt the pale brow, then he grasped the hand. "I believe he is!" His fingers sought the pulse. His sigh broke forth with joy. "The fever has broken; he is going to make it!"

It is unbelievable how news travels among the Chinese. Almost as soon as Rankin's words of relief and victory were uttered, a glad cry arose from below.

Waa I Saang would live!

Sam Rankin watched the hills of Wuchow recede as the Canton ferry plowed through the waters of the West River. Bill Wallace was on the road to recovery and now Sam, Everley Hayes, and Don Moore were returning to language school. "I still don't see how he pulled through," Sam said. "There was no earthly reason for it."

Everley smiled, "No earthly reason, true, but maybe there was a divine reason."

In the fall of that year, 1948, Bill Wallace, still thin but fully recovered, was back at work. He was no longer alone. The Rankins, the Galloways, and Everley Hayes had completed language training and moved to Wuchow. Bill was never happier.

Bill Wallace and Sam Rankin enjoyed working together. They made an excellent team. Bill's surgical prowess was a wonder to Sam, and he observed him carefully at every opportunity.

"Sam, come over here and meet my friend." Bill Wallace stood by a window with an incredibly filthy youngster. Sam recognized the tattered stripling as a beggar boy whom other boys in the neighborhood often mocked because of his deformity.

The Chinese boy's eyes darted fearfully from one doctor to the other. Life had not been kind to him. Victim of a congenital harelip and cleft palate, he roamed the streets unwanted, taunted, driven, unable to communicate his needs.

In the light from the window, Bill was looking at the deformed mouth. His hand gently cupped the boy's chin. "Let's fix him up, Sam. Let's give him a chance in life."

Rankin moved in for a closer look, and Bill asked, "Have you ever done one of these?"

"No, I never have," answered the new missionary.

"You do this one," Bill said. "I'll assist you."

Under Bill's guidance, Sam Rankin did his first harelip and cleft palate surgery. The result was beautiful, and the boy's eyes took on a new luster as he made his recovery and beheld his new countenance in the mirror. When he could make himself understood for the first time, he cried with joy. Sam was elated, and Bill was, in turn, excited to see the new physician's heart respond to the possibilities of a medical ministry in a place like Wuchow.

When the boy was pronounced healed and his rehabilitation satisfactory, he was discharged. Bill hired him as an orderly. He made a good one and was especially apt in reassuring fearful patients who faced surgery. Sam Rankin took note of Bill's interest and insight into the needs of the whole man.

Although Bill was only forty years old in 1948, he was a father to his staff. He was even asked more than once to stand up as father when one of them married. None of those present ever forgot a wedding that fall when an orphan girl, literally raised in the hospital and later trained as a nurse, was given in marriage.

Bill Wallace took the traditional role as if he indeed were her father. He arranged the details of the marriage contract, organized the prenuptial ceremonies, and with solemn dignity and poise signed the marital documents. At the wedding feast, he was a typical father-of-the-bride and enjoyed himself immensely. New missionaries marveled at the acceptance that was his among his adopted people.

With the enlarged staff to ease the hospital routine, Bill began to make more excursions into nearby villages with the evangelistic workers. In October he took a team to the little village of Hu Ching. They moved through the streets of Wuchow just before dawn, carrying medical supplies, food, clothing, Bibles, and gospel tracts. Bill owned a brand new plywood boat and a powerful outboard motor which constituted his chief recreation. He rigged up an awning and a towline for a sampan to carry the evangelistic team and supplies. Twelve workers, medical and evangelistic, volunteered for the trip.

It was barely dawn when they chugged out on the glassy West River for a ten-mile ride up the Fu River. The remainder of the trip had to be made on foot.

When they reached the Hu Ching trail, Dr. Wallace and his companions pulled the boats to the bank. Everyone loaded equipment on his back and climbed a towering green hill by a steep, narrow path. On the other side of the hill they gazed down into a peaceful valley and the little village that was their destination. As they started down the hill, children began running from the village to meet them. Soon they crowded about the missionaries shouting greetings. Several who had come to know him at the children's ward of the Stout Memorial Hospital literally threw themselves at Bill.

Bill loved these mission trips. He liked to walk into the village and greet the elders and ruffle the hair of the bright-eyed youngsters.

On these trips, the Wuchow workers distributed clothing, New Testaments, and tracts. Members of the evangelistic team went into the homes and spoke to people they had met on other trips. They also instructed new Christians and worked with the local pastor in examining new converts. While they were doing this work, Bill Wallace and Everley Hayes conducted a clinic in another part of the village. Most of the patients were mothers and children to whom they gave shots or whose sores they cleaned and dressed. As Bill worked, children crowded around him and asked questions. When he looked up and responded in his Cantonese with its Tennessee drawl, they laughed and ran off but soon came back. They loved him and watched wide-eyed as he worked with patients.

Later, the missionary team gathered together for a service that began with the children singing Christian hymns in Chinese. After a sermon and a closing prayer, the missionaries packed up to leave, and the children escorted them to the edge of town singing, "God Will Take Care of You." Its melody was still ringing from the village when the missionaries topped the green hill.

Christmas, 1948, was a warm and gay time for the missionaries in Wuchow and for the staff of the Stout Memorial Hospital. For one thing, Bill and the nurses now had a family. A child, whose mother had died in the hospital despite desperate efforts to save her, had been "adopted" by the compassionate missionary doctor. He named the youngster Paul, and, although the nurses did most of the caring for him, the doctor felt that in a very special way this was his charge.

Bill never failed to give some little gift to nearly everyone with whom he was in the slightest way related—and always to the chil-

dren in the hospital. With the presence of the Rankins and the
Galloways and especially the thoughtful, sunny Everley Hayes,
Christmas Eve was exciting. They gathered together for dinner,
just the missionary staff, at the home of the Rankins. The night
before, they had had their Christmas program at the hospital, with
the exchange of gifts and a visit to the chapel to give grateful
thanks. They followed this with a party on the hospital terrace with
choirs from the Baptist Bible school and the Alliance Bible school
singing Christmas songs along with the student nurses' choir.

The next morning, shortly after finishing his rounds at six o'clock,
Bill Wallace surprised Everley Hayes by suggesting that they go
over to "the Hill" to wish the Alliance folks a Merry Christmas. She
exclaimed, "But they won't even be up yet!" He replied with a
mischievous grin, "That's the whole idea."

After they had finished checking the night reports, they ambled
down the still, deserted Wuchow streets, caught a sampan across
the Fu River and climbed the hill to the Alliance station. Only the
dogs greeted them. Bill called a cheerful "Merry Christmas!" as
loud as he could, and lights began to come on all over the compound. The Newberns loved Bill as if he were a part of their family
and the feeling was quite mutual. Nothing would do but that they
stay for breakfast.

On January 17, the whole Baptist Mission and the group from
"the Hill" came to the Rankins' to celebrate Bill Wallace's forty-
first birthday. He had been in China for fourteen years. Everley
baked a birthday cake, and though the weather was gloomy and
very chilly—36 degrees that morning—they enjoyed kidding Bill
about being a bachelor at his age. The perennial topic was especially timely because of an incident that happened at one of the
feasts just before Christmas.

One of the Chinese, a close friend of Bill's, asked him for the
umpteenth time why he did not marry. Bill lightheartedly replied,
"Nobody will have me."

The Chinese friend, very concerned about this, inquired, "Would
you like for me to get you a wife?"

Bill just grunted, meaning to shrug away the whole question. The sound he made meant "yes" to the Chinese. To his chagrin, the Chinese friend appeared at the hospital the next day with a German-Chinese girl, a Eurasian, along with her mother, to arrange for a marriage with the renowned doctor. The distraught missionary realized what was happening when the mother came in and embraced him and began talking contract for the marriage.

Flushing and stammering, he said, "There must be some mistake."

She said, "Oh, no, I am quite sure there has been no mistake."

Suddenly, he remembered an emergency at the hospital and rushed away.

The mother returned often with her lovely daughter, but somehow she was unable to find Dr. Wallace. He went for many long walks in the hills those days. It was only after a careful explanation had been made by some of his friends (struggling to hold back their own hilarity over the situation) that the embarrassing incident was finally resolved.

The tranquil days at the mission following the close of the Japanese War passed swiftly. It seemed that they were only to be the eye of the storm. To the north, ominous clouds in the form of a giant Red specter were forming. Communism, Chinese-style, was on the march. The Communists were not strangers to Bill Wallace. They had been fighting Chiang Kai-shek and his Nationalists when Bill first came to China.

Communism, a Russian import, began in China in the early 1920's. From 1921 to 1927 the Communist Party, fed and nurtured by their comrades in Siberia, grew from fifty to sixty thousand and gained control of two million trade union workers and nine million peasants. In the days of Sun Yat-sen, they gained a voice in government.

When Chiang Kai-shek took over, however, he realized the dangerous nature of this alliance between his Kuomintang and the Communists, and he made a dramatic break with them. The Communists fought back, and the Generalissimo began an all-out liquidation campaign, which by 1936 was nearing success. Then the Reds pulled off their famous kidnapping of the Chinese leader, and this, together with the Japanese threat, enabled them to exact a treaty of coexistence from the man who a few days before seemed destined to purge them from China's soil.

Though the Japanese drive cut the Communists off from the rest of China, it gave them unlimited control of the northlands. There they fattened their armies, trained hordes of political workers, and began infiltration into the rest of China under the cover of war.

Wryly, Bill remembered how easily he dismissed the predictions Dr. Beddoe made when Russia, who conveniently joined the Japanese War a few days before it ended, turned over to the Chinese Reds Manchuria and the captured war materials. "We will live to regret this day," Beddoe had said.

When Nationalist troops were airlifted to the area, they found the Reds armed, fat, and waiting.

Early efforts by the United States to forestall the civil war (also deplored by the wise old Beddoe) only gave the Communists time to prepare further for their conquest. By late 1948 the issue was no longer in doubt. Despite last-ditch efforts by Chiang to correct corruption within his own ranks, deal with a devastating inflation, and stem the tide of defecting commanders, the Red dragon began to devour the land. It stopped only to digest what it had eaten.

The missionaries gathered on the hospital porch to watch the ushering in of the Chinese New Year, on January 28, 1949. Bill Wallace, Miss Hayes, and Miss Bradley were up until 2:00 A.M. with an obstetrical case, so they went back out on the porch to watch the latter part of the celebration. It continued into the wee hours of the morning. The fogs were forming on the river when Bill said, "I am afraid things are going to change drastically before we see another of these celebrations."

In early spring, the Nationalist capital at Nanking and Chiang Kai-shek moved to Canton. Since the Chinese Communists demanded unconditional surrender, the last hopes for negotiations passed. It was a confused situation. The missionaries—feeling a part of it all and yet not a part of it—looked with dismay upon the swirling tides. Prayerfully, they girded themselves for whatever might be ahead.

14

One Piece of Man

It was spring of 1949, and Kweilin was threatened, Shanghai would soon fall, and the Red drive toward Canton was making unexpected progress. The word from missionaries who were trying to stay on in territory now dominated by the Communists was not encouraging.

Ed Galloway and Bill Wallace decided to risk a trip to Hong Kong before the rainy season arrived. They needed to pick up an elevator a church back home had shipped to the hospital. It was a dangerous trip because advance Communist elements were now being seen along the West River. One week before, Ed had made the same trip and, upon his return voyage, Communist shots rained down from the adjoining hills. Ed had looked up to find the man next to him dead, shot through the head.

As they approached the danger area on this trip, one of the ferry's crew members came up to Ed. "Are you with him?" The man was pointing at Bill Wallace, seated low against a railing, watching the foreboding banks.

Puzzled, Ed replied, "Yes, I am. Why do you ask?"

"The captain desires both of you to come to his cabin," the man said. "Please follow me."

Catching Bill's eye and motioning for him to come along, Ed followed. Inside the captain's spacious quarters, the crewman asked them to wait and excused himself. In a moment the captain entered. He addressed himself to Ed.

"Your traveling companion," the captain nodded toward the smiling Wallace, "has saved my worthless life three times. Yet, he has refused me the opportunity to repay him. Now you are my guests and I want you to share my meal with me. You see, you will be safe here if the Communists fire upon us again."

121

Smiling, the captain pointed to an armored dome over the cabin. "This way I shall repay the good doctor."

"Well, I'll declare!" exclaimed Ed, turning to look at Bill.

A bit embarrassed by the whole thing, Bill grinned, shrugged his shoulders, then quipped, "I was hoping to get credit for this one in heaven, but it looks as if we had better take it now."

They enjoyed the captain's hospitality immensely, and when a few random shots plowed into the boat a half hour later, they were grateful for the Chinese skipper's sense of honor.

Upon returning to Wuchow, Bill and Ed were met by a missionary couple from the hospital in Kweilin who were on their way to Hong Kong. They reported that the Communists were nearing Kweilin, and from all they could hear, prospects for continued service under Communist rule were not good. The disturbed couple had decided to return to the United States.

The next few days were filled with rumors that the Nationalists had surrendered, that the Communists were within miles of the city. While Bill and his fellow missionaries knew this was false, they were sobered when they received word from the American consul in Canton advising all Americans to leave South China as soon as possible. They realized it was time to take a hard look at the future.

Baker James Cauthen was now area secretary in the Orient for the Southern Baptist Foreign Mission Board. The former Kweilin missionary had succeeded Theron Rankin, who had become executive secretary upon Dr. Maddry's retirement. In May, Cauthen called a mission meeting in Canton to study the threatening situation. Bill Wallace and his fellow missionaries in Wuchow selected Ed Galloway to go as their representative.

When Ed returned from the meeting, they gathered in Sam Rankin's living room to hear his report. Dr. Cauthen's statement had been simple and to the point, Ed stated. The area secretary shared decisions already made by missionaries in the north and something of what those who had elected to stay in Communist areas were experiencing. All were finding it difficult, but some felt it was worth trying.

Now they must decide to stay, to return home, or to transfer to another field. Cauthen pointed out that negotiations were under way to begin work in several new areas. Whatever they decided, the Board would back them completely. If they chose to stay, it must be because they definitely felt it was what God would have them to do. There was to be no time limit on decisions, though undoubtedly the advancing Communist tide made some kind of decision imminent. After prayer for God's leadership, they had dispersed to return to their stations.

When Ed concluded his report of the meeting, the missionaries were silent for a moment. Then Bill spoke quietly, but firmly.

"This cannot be a station decision; it must be made individually. Each of us will have unique considerations and each must decide now to respect the other's conclusion, no matter what it is."

It was the only approach to take. In the days that followed they gradually made their choices. For some, the right course seemed clearly evident; for others, it came only after much prayer and agonizing appraisal of all involved.

During this time, they listened carefully for word coming from other areas and the decisions others were making. At some stations, the missionaries were asked by their Chinese brethren to leave. They held no hostility toward these apostles in their midst, but there was the possibility that the presence of foreigners would actually hinder their cause. News from areas already overrun seemed to bear out the wisdom of this in some cases. If the Chinese Christians in Wuchow felt this way, they did not share it with the Americans at this time. Had they done so, it might have made some decisions easier.

Bill announced his decision first. He would stay. Too much was at stake to leave the hospital at this time and he was the logical person to stay with it.

Blanche Bradley was near retirement. Trained for Mandarin-speaking work and unable to speak the Cantonese dialect very well, she felt she would only be a hindrance. She would go.

Ed and Betty Galloway decided to go. An opportunity was open for them to begin work in Thailand among the Chinese populace and they felt they should take it. Their missionary career was just beginning and they longed for a more stable situation.

Though Jessie Green was due a furlough, she elected to postpone it for the present and try to stay on. Her work was flourishing and she felt if she left at this time, she might not be able to get back in later.

Everley Hayes shared her decision with Bill after surgery one day. "I'm going to stay on, Bill. The hospital needs a missionary nurse and I'm just now getting to where I can handle the language pretty well."

Bill smiled at his determined colleague. "I figured you would, Everley." Then, more seriously, he added, "You're sure this is what you really want to do? It may get pretty rough."

"I'm sure," she said. "I'm real sure."

Sam and Miriam Rankin finally made a difficult decision to go. Their youngest child needed a type of surgery done best in the States. They would go and hope another opportunity would open later.

That was it; five would go, three would stay. There was warm support for each decision.

The Galloways were the first to depart. The day they left on the ferry for Hong Kong, Bill and Ed walked up the hill back of the hospital.

"I know this is what we should do, Bill. The prospects at Bangkok sound good. The thing that bothers me is leaving you and Everley and Jessie. Now and then, I wonder if I'm running out on you."

Bill replied, "No. I definitely feel you are doing the right thing. You have a family, and you must take their well-being into consideration. If you stayed, you would be beset with worries for them, and you would not be able to do the job you will be free to do in Thailand. With me, it's different. I'm the one to stay. I'm just one piece of man without other responsibilities."

One piece of man—it was an old Chinese saying used courteously to depreciate one's value. It indicated a single, unencumbered, expendable person. By it, Bill meant his life was the only one at stake. He was the one thus seated by circumstances, prepared by God for this moment. He was the one to stay on in the face of the unknown, to give the Stout Memorial Hospital and the Baptist witness every chance to continue living, once the Red blight arrived.

"I'm just one piece of man . . .," Ed Galloway repeated the conversation to his wife as the ferry carried them to Hong Kong. "He really meant it. He has no concept of his own worth and no anxiety for the future that I can see."

A few days later one of the Catholic missionaries dropped by the hospital for some medicine and stopped to visit with his good friend, Bill Wallace.

"They tell me you are going to try to stay on, Bill."

"Why, yes, Father. You people are staying, aren't you?"

"True, but then we are expendable," the priest jested.

"Well, somebody has to stay to look after you." They laughed together, thankful for an opportunity to relax the growing tension. There was nothing heroic in Bill's decision. He felt the same sense of duty he had felt when the Japanese were storming through South China five years before.

Soon it was time for the Rankins and Miss Bradley to leave. Their leave-taking was poignantly subdued; the women wept softly as the men shook hands quietly. They had enjoyed working together and wished the situation were different, that the fruitful days of their short co-ministry could continue.

"Maybe someday, Bill."

"God willing, Sam. Take care of yourself and take care of my little girl for me." Bill was extremely fond of the golden-haired tot they were taking home for surgery.

Bill, Everley, and Jessie stood at the dock until they lost sight of the ferry around the bend. Then, silently, they walked back to the hospital.

Their sadness was compounded two weeks later when William Newbern walked over to the Baptist compound to tell Bill that the Orient secretary for the Missionary Alliance group had ordered them to proceed to Hong Kong. After the Newbern family left, Bill found it hard to look across the river at the deserted station on the hill without a pang of nostalgia.

But there was much to do. Hospital occupancy was high and

they were handicapped by an exodus of nursing students returning to their homes because of the impending crisis. Bill began to purchase vital supplies to be stored against the time when they would not have access to outside markets. The Bamboo Curtain had already descended in North China. South China could expect the same fate.

Then nature contrived to complicate matters. The West and Fu Rivers went on a rampage in early July, 1949, and were soon lapping at the foundations of their old victim, Wuchow. Bill had to wade through water ankle-deep to get to church on the second Sunday in July. When the worshipers came out, the water had climbed to the top steps. Bill took a sampan back to the hospital.

By evening the water was at the doors of the clinic and Bill knew they were in for the worst inundation in his sixteen years in China. The next morning they discontinued using the clinic and moved the equipment up to the hospital.

The muddy water stretched from the hospital grounds all the way to the distant pagoda on the far side of the valley, and much of Wuchow now rested beneath its swirling tides. Beddoe had always said it would never reach the hospital steps, and just as Bill decided the old prophet was going to be wrong for a change, the waters began to recede.

The retreating flood left a trail of destruction in its wake: mud, slime, crumpled homes, mangled trees, and disease. But the Chinese had crawled out of such disasters before to rebuild, and this time was no exception. At the hospital, Bill faced the problem of no water—their well had caved in; no electricity, and a stream of flood victims seeking treatment. But the demanding days were in a sense a blessing as it took minds off the inexorable Communist advance.

After the flood, the South China Mission decided to have its regular mission meeting in Canton despite the small number of missionaries left. Fortunately, the unusual floods temporarily halted the Red tide for a time. Bill, Everley, and Jessie all decided to attend the meeting as it would be the last opportunity to visit with their fellow missionaries. The prospect brightened their days. On the day they were to leave, however, Bill was faced with emergency surgery and he had to send the women on alone. He was severely disappointed, but there was no question as to where he belonged. He wrote a brief note for Everley to take to Gene and Louise Hill, who were among those staying in Canton. It might be a long time before he got to see them again.

Bill worked steadily while his nurse-helpers were at the mission conference. On the afternoon they were to return he decided to meet their plane. As he started to his bungalow for a shower and change of clothes, he saw the hospital business manager running up the path.

"Waa I Saang! Waa I Saang!"

"What's the problem, Chan?"

"Word has come that the Communists shot down the Canton plane about a half hour ago! The pilot radioed they were being attacked and there has been no further communication."

Bill's heart pounded. "O God, please let them be all right." He was not sure he could take it if anything happened to Everley and Jessie. He started toward the gate on the run.

"Where are you going?" Mr. Chan called.

"Down to customs; they may know something," he shouted back.

At customs, they had confirmed that the plane had indeed been downed. First word from the scene said all on board were lost. They were trying to get a passenger list from Canton now.

Bill sat down to wait, praying over and over again, "God, let them be safe."

Two hours later, customs still did not have the passenger list, but Bill was standing up with tears running down his cheeks, reading a telegram Chan had brought him.

"Missed plane. Will come by ferry on Monday." It was signed EVERLEY and JESSIE. They arrived safely on Monday.

After mission meeting, Baker James Cauthen decided to make one last visit to the South China stations that would soon be cut off by the Communists. Despite the danger, he and his secretary, Lucy Smith, booked passage on the seaplane to Wuchow.

On the trip from Hong Kong to Wuchow, Dr. Cauthen peered out upon the familiar South China landscape with its contrasting shades of green and brown and wondered how long he and those whom he was going to visit would continue to serve there. For a second time in a decade the ravages of war threatened to engulf them—first, the Japanese; now, the Communists. How much time was left? Three weeks? Three months? The inevitable triumph of the Peiping regime was a foregone conclusion. Memories of the incredible reports from North China furrowed his brow with concern for the days ahead.

He was eager to see the tall Tennessean. For some reason Bill Wallace always reminded him of the silent actor, Gary Cooper. Even Cooper's famous "Yep" was a mouthful for Wallace. Cauthen admired Wallace's determination not to be driven out by the Communists, "to stay as long as I can serve," but he found himself breathing a prayer for Bill's safety. Then the seat belt sign flashed on, and he realized they were approaching Wuchow.

He stepped forth to be greeted by the three Wuchow missionaries. Bill hollered in his brand of Cantonese, "Taxi, mister?"

Laughing, Cauthen threw his raincoat and briefcase into Bill's boat and then helped Lucy Smith as they tried to balance themselves in the small craft. Bill, Everley, and Jessie inquired eagerly about the Rankins, Miss Bradley, and the Galloways, and were grateful to receive assurances that all received passage home. Bill said, "They did a good job here, but this is no place for a family."

Later that evening while waiting for the others, Dr. Cauthen stood alone on the porch of the old Beddoe house. He watched a red glow crown the hospital as the sun set on the hills beyond. The brown stones took on a ruddy softness.

Steps turned his attention to the walk. Everley Hayes, in a crisp white uniform, was coming from her apartment. The reds and blues in the garden behind her formed a colorful background.

"Well," he said, "you don't look like you have been on duty all day."

She shook her head and said, "I have, and all night too. A soldier came in yesterday with gangrene. He had walked over a hundred miles. We tried all night to save him, and I think we have succeeded."

"That's wonderful!" Cauthen replied. Then, turning to look at the hospital again, he said, "Don't they call it 'The Life of China'?"

Just then, Bill Wallace loped around the corner, stethoscope flopping from his coat. Cauthen, noting that the young doctor seemed always on the run, joked, "Dr. Wallace, I presume."

Everley laughed and quipped, "You ought to feel honored, Dr. Cauthen. When Bill shows up for any meal other than Sunday dinner, it must be an occasion."

Wallace looked hurt in the best silent movie tradition and then said, "It has been a long time since Sunday. Let's eat!"

After dinner, the missionaries, with Dr. Cauthen, sat on the porch and discussed some of the problems they soon would face.

"One of the most sobering aspects of staying on is that you will not have the protection of the American consul. Our Government will not recognize the Peiping regime." Dr. Cauthen made the statement slowly and then paused to let it sink in.

Bill asked, "Are the Communists confiscating American property yet?"

"They have not taken over any mission property as such, but they are making more and more demands in some areas," Cauthen answered. "In one place, local Communist authorities are asking to hold the title and let our missionaries 'use' the property free gratis."

"That sounds to me as if they intend to take it over," Jessie said.

"They may be planning to do just that," the secretary replied. "But, if we remain firm, they might hold off for a while to avoid unfavorable world opinion."

Bill Wallace, sitting on the concrete floor with his back resting against the cool wall, looked at the beloved old hospital, then asked, "Would we fare better if we turned the property over to the Leung Kwang Baptist Convention? Perhaps the Communists would be less disposed to take it over then."

This action had long been Robert Beddoe's dream and his successor had often pondered its merits.

"In the long pull, that might be the best action, but right now foreign property holders are faring better than the Chinese," Cauthen responded.

He did not have to spell this out. Already, stories of the whole-sale purges and slaughter of landlords in the North were seeping out to a shocked world.

"Ultimately, it's the Lord's property," Cauthen continued, "and we will have to trust that he will use it for his glory, come what may."

They nodded at the wisdom of these words. Bill added, "And ultimately, we are his people. Even without the American consul, we always have the Lord."

The next day, Bill, Everley, Jessie, and many of the Chinese Baptist leaders saw Cauthen and Lucy Smith to their plane for their return to Hong Kong. As Dr. Cauthen shook Bill's hand firmly, he said, "Remember, Bill, there are going to be a lot of people pray-ing for you in the coming months."

"We're counting on it." Bill smiled.

Now began the long wait.

Bill Wallace had the advantage, if it could be called that, of having sweated out the steady advance of an enemy before. He tried to reassure Everley and Jessie, but he knew from experience that nothing would totally eliminate the simmering anxiety of the unknown.

In Wuchow, Communist political workers were restlessly infiltrat-ing every area of life. From their "underground" headquarters, they boasted of their readiness to take control of the city. They used fear on one hand and suave assurances on the other to further con-found the already demoralizing situation. It was especially hard on the Christians who knew that the Communist ideology was lethally opposed to all for which they stood. Many of the leaders were weighing whether or not to leave.

Bill and all the church leaders were dealt a severe blow when one of the hospital Bible women, long a faithful worker, was caught in adultery. The Communist propagandists pounced upon this to discredit the hospital and the Christians. Yet, in the midst of the scandal, the Wuchow Baptists experienced one of their most fruitful seasons and baptized nineteen new converts a week after the scandal broke. It was as if God had chosen their weakest moment, humanly speaking, to display his effective power in men's lives. Bill, Everley, and Jessie drew strength from the turn of events.

To try to relieve the increasing tension among the hospital staff, Bill suggested regular outings and recreation periods. Again and again, he hitched up an old sampan to the back of his boat and hauled the student nurses and staff members upriver to Chicken Basket Island for a picnic and swim. He even rigged up a water sled to pull for the younger, more vigorous staff members. The doctor laughingly maneuvered the boat in exaggerated efforts to throw them.

But his efforts to keep their minds off the approaching Red plague were only partially successful. Discipline problems arose and nearly every day more students pulled out to return home or flee the country with their families. There seemed to be no remission from the gnawing malignancy of fear.

At the end of the summer a child close to death with malaria was brought into the hospital. A student nurse quickly gave the little boy a shot of quinine, but it was too late and he died as they worked over him. Though the child would have died anyway, the parents felt it was the hospital's fault, and with loud wails and dark threats, they prepared to sue the hospital.

In China, doctors and hospitals had very little legal protection, and they could easily be sued and made to pay fines of fantastic proportions. A hospital administrator had to be as "wise as a serpent and as harmless as a dove." Bill did not like such tasks, but he tried to meet them head-on.

The family asked for $3,000 Hong Kong money. Bill said they would not be able to collect anything if they went to court, but since he knew they had sustained a loss and were hurt, he would try to see if something could be done for them. He could not pay the money through the hospital, for that would be the same as admitting the hospital's guilt. Working with the business manager of the hospital, he arranged to have the family paid through another source. It was complicated and distasteful to the young doctor, and he returned to his surgical responsibilities with relief.

The Communists were now advancing up the West River. By

the last of October, people of Wuchow were in a panic. Shops that ordinarily stayed open until nine o'clock at night started closing before sundown. People on the streets became fewer and thieves became bolder. The town still housed a large group of Nationalist soldiers—many of them dwelling in tents by the river, others in old fortifications in the hills—but the many local Communists worked overtime spreading discord and rumors in preparation for the inevitable take-over.

Rumors floated everywhere, and there were always those ready to believe them. Fear plowed the ground and made it easier for the seed to take root and grow.

One night Bill heard that the hospital was going to be robbed by a large band of thieves, and he was urged to hide everything of value. He replied that there was little use to do so. Things hidden could always be found, or people could be tortured to tell. Nevertheless, Bill spent that night in the hospital, a lonesome guard. Nothing happened, but the panic grew.

Refugees were coming in from Canton and other cities that had fallen to the Communists. They, along with Nationalist troops in retreat, made a steady procession through the town to the West. Evacuation plans were passed out by the Nationalist officials, but the hospital staff notified the officials that they would not evacuate. Knowing that Dr. Wallace was going to stay made some of the people feel better.

By the end of October, Bill and Everley had no choice but to dismiss the nursing classes, although they had just received the government registration for which they had waited a long time. They had only two students left. The night they closed classes they heard on the radio that Kweilin to the northwest had been lost. That loss meant that Wuchow was the last Southern Baptist mission station in all China that was still unoccupied by Reds.

It had been five and a half months since the Rankins and Galloways and Miss Bradley left Wuchow. At that time, many thought it would be only a matter of weeks until the Communists took over. Now, at a meeting of the hospital staff, a doctor asked Dr. Wallace how long it would be. Bill said they could count on one month. He was right, to the very day. The Communists were just hours from Wuchow on Thanksgiving Day, 1949.

Everley and Jessie fixed a traditional meal, and then the three missionaries sat out on the porch to talk. Rumors said the Nationalist troops were to pull out that night. One had it that they planned to burn the city rather than turn it over to the Communists. The citizens feared fire and robbery more than anything else, but for the missionaries, the big fear was the over-all uncertainty of the next few hours and days.

Everley mused out loud. "It is a funny feeling, this waiting. It is sort of a detached feeling, as though we are not really a part of it, but just onlookers."

"The thing that bothers me most," said Jessie, "is the fear in the faces of the people."

"I know," replied Bill. "Mr. Chan came by this morning and said he had finally decided he must take his family out. He was going to stay, but today he looked pale with fear."

Far below them a column of Nationalist troops filed through the streets. They could hear the iron shoes of the pack mules clanking on the cobblestones.

"Listen." Bill cupped a hand to his ear. They heard the unmistakable chatter of machine gun bursts. "I believe we had better wait this one out at the hospital. We can watch from the roof."

Closing the house, they ran to the old building and mounted the steps to the roof. There Bill pointed to the hill to their left.

"I don't see anything." Everley strained her eyes in the direction he pointed. Then tracer bullets arched into the town from a clump of bamboo, and she saw running, crouching Communist soldiers moving into Wuchow.

Two hours later, long columns of the green-uniformed soldiers were winding into the city. Their tennis shoes topped by winding putties hardly disturbed the silence or scuffed the dust. From the front of their soft caps, with earlaps tied over the top, gleamed a red star.

Wuchow, the Stout Memorial Hospital, and the three Southern Baptist missionaries were behind the Bamboo Curtain.

15

The Bamboo Curtain

Life under the Communists was relatively uncomplicated in the beginning. True to their pattern elsewhere, they endeavored first to gain the people's confidence. Though immediate organization under the People's Party began, most of the populace—including the missionaries themselves—were lulled into a false sense of security.

A real scare came to the hospital staff, however, the day following the Communist take-over. Bill was called out of surgery when a large contingent of soldiers started up the road toward the hospital. He met them at the clinic to learn that they were demanding to be housed in the hospital. He politely pointed out that patients were housed in the hospital, and that the staff were not authorized to run a boarding house. When the officer in charge, however, made a few thinly veiled threats, Bill agreed to furnish them temporary space on the first floor.

The nurses, especially those sleeping in the single nurses' quarters, were frightened, and so Everley moved in with them from her house in the compound. She was not sure what protection she would be, but it seemed to give them confidence. Bill moved a cot to the top of the steps between the first and second floors. Any of his "boarders" would have to step over him to get to the second floor.

Resolute, but not belligerent, Bill's manner bespoke courage and commanded the respect of the soldiers. Too, they were under orders to be on their best behavior. The Communists used courtesy to good advantage during these early days as they moved into areas beset by all the problems of disorganized and often corrupt administration. The contingent of soldiers stayed at the hospital only one night and then moved on.

"It's impossible." Everley Hayes was indignant. As Bill Wallace came up to the nurse's desk, he noticed her determined stance with her eyes flashing and her hands on her hips. She was talking to a minor official of the new Wuchow administration.

"What's the matter, Everley?"

"This man wants me to send ten nurses in full uniform to a parade in one hour. I can't do it; I'm shorthanded as it is. We're a hospital, not a marching unit."

The official smiled, but his smile was forced and icy. "This hospital must co-operate with the People's Party if it expects the Party to sanction it and protect it. Your co-operation will prove your goodwill."

Everley started to reply, but Bill restrained her. Then he said, "Our hospital will be represented in the parade."

The official bowed and departed. As he left, Everley turned to the doctor, obviously puzzled. "Where in the world . . .?" She did not finish.

He grinned and said, "Send four nurses. We can cover for them for a few hours, and we do want to show our goodwill."

"He said ten!" she protested.

"But I only said we would be represented . . ."

"Shhh!" Everley stopped the doctor and waited for an orderly to move by. He had been furiously dusting only a few feet away.

"I don't trust that new orderly any further than I can throw him. He always listens in on everything, and he is giving the nurses the creeps. Do you think he could be here as an informer?" Everley asked the question cautiously, a bit fearfully.

Bill rubbed his chin thoughtfully. "Maybe, Everley. They seem to have infiltrated everything and everyplace. Chan says the walls now have ears. Let's make it a point to be sure we're alone when we are referring to anything political."

The next day they read in the paper of a "spontaneous parade" held in Wuchow as proof of the new government's popularity. Mass meetings were interspersed with the "spontaneous" demonstrations. The Baptist church was commandeered for such a gathering one Wednesday afternoon shortly before its members were to meet for prayer. The distraught pastor came to Bill and the latter accompanied him to the church. Bill explained to an official that a regular meeting was scheduled there. The official assured him that it would be available at the time for their meeting.

The noisy meeting adjourned as promised at the time for prayer, and the waiting worshipers entered and began their meeting. But they met in the midst of screaming posters, ostensibly from the Communist rally, but pointedly left:

"China for the Chinese." "Foreigners Have Ruined China." "Chiang Kai-shek, the Butcher, Is a Foreign Dupe."

As the members bowed for prayer, no one mentioned the signs.

Life had changed for Bill and his fellow missionaries, but more in atmosphere than routine. Their routine was the same: to heal and serve in the name of their Lord. And the demanding parade of those needing what they had to offer did not slack.

Christmas that year (1949) was a subdued affair. Jessie, Everley, and Bill gathered in the girls' quarters for a private Christmas dinner. It was a great contrast to the previous Christmas, when they had all been so gay. They had less to eat this time, but by thrift and ingenuity, they managed roast chicken, potatoes, and ice cream. There was no real shortage of food during those weeks, but they did not feel free to go out and do much purchasing. During dinner, even Bill was extremely talkative (for him), trying to cheer up the others and create a festive atmosphere. Afterward, they knelt together in prayer.

The New Year brought more Communist festivities, with everyone expected to participate. Despite Everley's protests, her nursing staff was taken again and again for demonstrations. Her students were also commandeered for indoctrination courses. Some of the nurses left the hospital to join the youth corps organized by the Communists, and others too obviously became indoctrinated by their propaganda. This state of affairs strained things among those who were loyal to their Christian faith and who did not feel they could reject their God to accept the Party line.

Now the public trials began. First, only the most obvious tyrants were brought to trial. But the people were being schooled in a new type of trial—a trial by mob. They were commanded to appear before large open-air courts. Led by stooges spotted throughout the crowd, they learned to respond with cries and yells on signal.

The first trials in South China were for those guilty of the crime of being a landlord. Crowds were convened for the trials early in the morning and whipped into a frenzy by their singing Communist songs and chanting slogans.

When the landlords were brought up from jail, they were greeted by crowds with drums and cymbals who marched them along like animals in a circus parade. Their hands were tied behind their backs to make them look more like criminals, and cone-shaped dunce caps were placed on their heads.

Trials began with long speeches on democracy, the will of the people, and the judgment of the people. Then the accusers came. Often they were women who screamed and yelled the crimes of the landlords. The leader asked the mob after each accusation, "Is that just?" The mob yelled "NO!" The leader then shouted, "Should he be punished?" The crowd screamed, "YES!"

In the midst of this madness, the gospel of Christ was preached at Stout Memorial Hospital. The tender ministrations of Bill Wallace and his staff, dedicated to mercy rather than to murder and to peace rather than to rioting, seemed marked in contrast. But the conditions under which they worked grew more and more difficult. Bill tried to keep busy in the clinic with medical experiments and with surgery. He had an unusual number of stomach ulcer cases. Tension was mounting, and fear was taking its toll.

Word came of more missionaries leaving. Eugene Hill became seriously ill with a hemorrhaging ulcer and was ordered out of China. After weeks of waiting for an exit permit, he and his wife and small son made their way to Hong Kong and back to the States. Bill breathed a prayer of gratitude when he heard they were safely out.

Then the Wuchow Christians suggested that Jessie should leave. While Everley and Bill were involved primarily in medicine, Jessie was involved strictly in evangelism. It was becoming so difficult to hold Christian meetings that they advised Jessie to leave for her own good as well as for theirs. She reluctantly applied for her permit to leave, and when after several weeks it was granted, she made her way out. This left only Bill Wallace and Everley Hayes.

It was a trying time for the doctor and his nurse, and while they needed each other's company more than ever before, they actually had less opportunity to be together than before the Communists came. They were able to be together only in social functions with others present because of the quickness on the part of the Communists to accuse foreigners of immorality or avarice at the slightest opportunity. Thus, Bill and Everley "avoided all appearance of evil." Except for dinners with the staff, they took their meals separately and met only in terms of the routine of the hospital. They understood the necessity for it and they were willing to pay the price to keep from clouding their witness to these people.

But one day Bill Wallace walked out of intricate surgery, peeled off his rubber gloves, laid aside his operating gown, and asked his fellow worker to go for a walk along the river. She knew why he had chosen that particular time. It was still before three o'clock in the afternoon and for about three hours there would be much activity along the streets and the riverbanks and the roads. There would be no opportunity for them to be out of anybody's sight, to give anyone reason to talk.

Smiling, she said, "Let's go."

At first they just walked quietly. Everley noticed that Bill was beginning to show his forty years for the first time. His hair had thinned, and since his brush with death three years previously, he had kept it clipped short. Now there was a hint of gray in it. Lines creased his forehead, and the corners of his eyes which had so often been creased by grinning, even now, with so little to grin about, held the hint of a grin. Things were more subdued, but daily activities in the streets of Wuchow had not really changed.

Lean, brown boys, their straining leg muscles sharply defined and glistening in the sun, still pushed down the streets crude-wheeled carts piled high with sacks of grain or charcoal. Red paper lanterns scrawled with advertising still hung in store fronts to welcome customers. Coolies under umbrella-shaped hats still quick-stepped along with baskets suspended at each end of long poles balanced on their shoulders. The smell of dried fish still filled the air, and, since it was summertime, the smell was strong. The Chinese wore their black summer suits of silk lacquered on the outside. They contrasted sharply with the white uniforms of the two missionaries who walked among them.

The missionaries walked by the Baptist True Light Book Store, now closed by the Communists. They saw an emblazoned Communist banner across the front of the church. It was going to be used for a Communist rally denouncing something or someone else, no doubt. Dusty-legged old men with white beards and pale eyes crouched behind baskets of dried persimmons along the road, eating with chopsticks and glancing disinterestedly at the Americans.

At the edge of town, the missionaries walked along the riverbank, every now and then coming under towering bamboo or great banyan trees. Boatloads of wood floated along the river, and smaller boats closer to shore moved in aimless patterns. Both missionaries noticed that people did not talk to them as readily as they once had. Yet, some whom Bill had treated at the hospital waved briefly.

The two kept walking. Farther up the river toward Cheung-Chou Island, they passed a little group of shacks with children playing in the front. Bill grinned at the children and they returned his smiles until an older one spoke loudly from behind a fence made of crates, "Look out for the foreign devils!" Then the children scattered.

All this time they had been quiet, but now Bill began to talk. He talked as if he knew things were drawing to a close. "You know, Everley, someday we will have done all we can do here and we may have to look for another place to work."

She nodded and pulled at a young bamboo stalk beside the walk.

"I have been doing a lot of thinking about it lately, and it seems to me there are some places where medical missionaries could be the key to some otherwise locked doors," Bill continued.

Reaching down, he picked up a rock and with a deft flip of the wrist flicked it out into the river. He laughed at himself as he remembered doing that before. It seemed a long time ago and a long way off.

"I have been thinking about the South Sea Islands. Java, Sumatra, Borneo are all places where a medical missions program might be used to begin Baptist work. I think a hospital can get us into areas that we cannot enter otherwise. It is said that Peter Parker opened China at the point of his lancet. Southern Baptists are going to go into those other areas someday. They are going to have to have someplace to put all the China missionaries. And, I'm not quite ready to retire yet."

Everley grinned at him. He still looked young, despite the signs of age that had so recently appeared. She could not think of him as at the end of his ministry—by retirement or anything else.

"Yes, I think we could begin a good work in that area," she said. "Maybe we could get Sam and Miriam Rankin and Betty and Ed Galloway to help us out there."

At the thought of their departed colleagues, they fell silent, and the conversation lagged. When she spoke again, Everley turned to their immediate plans.

The staff needed some diversion. With tension building up all around them and yet so much being required of them in terms of the hospital's services, Bill admitted it would be good to get away. They decided on another boat trip; Bill would take his boat and pull a good-sized barge that would carry all the staff that could be spared. They would take along the surfboard and a lot of fried chicken and find a good swimming place. Thus resolved, they returned to the compound, to their separate residences and their ever-demanding responsibilities.

The outing went off well. Everyone was looking for something to help them quit thinking about that which surrounded them. Many of the nurses were finding themselves torn between Communist propaganda and the Christian doctrines of the hospital and the missionaries that meant so much to them.

Bill enjoyed himself. He operated the boat when the others were surfboarding. When they were swimming, he lay on the bank lazily scratching the back of his dog's neck, his thoughts far away.

16

"For to Me to Live Is Christ"

The crisis which came in July, 1950, seemed to be related directly to the Korean conflict. When the North Korean invasion of South Korea began, Communist propaganda accused American imperialists as the real villains. Despite the fact the North Koreans had begun the attack, the South Koreans and their American allies were pictured as aggressors, murderers, ravagers. This propaganda affected Dr. Wallace and Everley Hayes and all who were associated with them.

When the United Nations entered the conflict in late July, the situation became even more precarious. New sets of regulations were published by the Communists. Tolerance and restraint began to disappear—they had served their purpose—and now the real face of communism was being revealed.

The new look started wholesale arrests. Guilty or suspect, masses of people were thrown into jail and heads began to roll.

Bill Wallace received a group of Chinese Communist officials who notified him of a grievous tax to be imposed upon the hospital. Deciding that acquiescence, even if the hospital could afford to pay, would be playing into Communist hands, he steadfastly refused. He said he would appeal it to their supervisors, that it was illegal, that he did not believe the People's Government would so handicap an institution bent only on a mission of mercy. He knew better, but his insistence threw them off guard.

Fearing that if something were not done they would lose their beloved Waa I Saang, local citizens gathered a petition from leading people of Wuchow and carried it to the People's Government headquarters at Canton. The Communists there evidently felt the time was not yet ripe for a showdown. They granted an exemption from the tax.

141

But the local Communists and their superiors in Canton were now aware of the influence of the slim American doctor who was so popular among the people of South China. The Communists were planning their invasion of Korea in support of the North Koreans and in direct opposition to the Americans and the United Nations. In early fall a hate-America campaign reached fantastic proportions in Wuchow.

At rallies, scathing denunciations of America and American "exploiters" were sounded with venom and malice: Yankee dogs, imperialist wolves, capitalistic dogs. The problem with this strategy in Wuchow was that the only American most of these Chinese knew was Bill Wallace. His life and the impact of his ministry made the charges against America and Americans seem incredible to them. Was not this an American hospital that had ministered so long to the people of Wuchow? Had not these Americans, despite risk and danger to themselves, identified themselves with the people, rich and poor? Was not Bill Wallace an American, the finest surgeon in all China, the hero of the Japanese War, the lover of their children, the self-effacing one who had lived among them above reproach for fifteen years?

The councils of evil began to seek ways and means to undermine this influence which negated their carefully planned propaganda. Finally, it was decided that the only way to discredit the hospital and the American Christians it represented was to discredit the man who, in the eyes of most people, was the hospital—Dr. Bill Wallace. How long before its actual revelation their plans were completed is not known. It is known that the last vestige of restraint disappeared in early December when China joined the Korean War. The purge and liquidation that followed cannot be detailed here, but what happened to Bill Wallace was no isolated incident.

The evening of December 18, Bill Wallace completed his rounds at the hospital as usual. A young Communist soldier whose ruptured appendix had been removed the night before seemed to be making satisfactory recovery, but Bill checked anyway. An elderly woman from whom he had removed a gallstone two days before was holding her own. The doctor stopped by the night nurse's desk and jotted down some instructions for special care. No matter how full the hospital, he assumed primary responsibility for every patient's welfare.

Stretching his long frame, he yawned, rubbed his eyes, excused himself, and walked into the chill night air. At the gate of the clinic he stopped and looked out over the blinking lights of Wuchow. It had rained at intervals most of the day, and a misty fog made an eerie specter of the whole scene. Bill could not quite shake it off, a sense of impending disaster.

Though the hospital had secured registration, he was not sure how much that would mean with the Communists' continued confiscation of foreign property and institutions of all kinds. Now that the Chinese were at war with the United Nations—and that meant America—how long could the mission hospital be allowed to serve unmolested? Perhaps it was time to leave China. He turned and looked back to the lights of the hospital that gleamed over the city as lights of hope. Still he had opportunity to heal and alleviate suffering. Could he run out on that?

He started over to see Miss Hayes and the senior nurse, Miss Luk, but, suddenly realizing how exhausted he was, he returned to his bungalow. He expected to be called during the night for a troublesome obstetrical case and decided to sleep while he could.

The doctor's devoted housekeeper saw his beloved Waa I Saang approaching. How weary he looked; his shortcropped hair was gray in the twilight and the lines of his face were accentuated. The houseboy experienced a deep feeling of concern for the doctor who so seldom thought of himself.

"Hello, Rastus [it was a nickname of unknown origin]. It's a good day for ducks." It occurred to Bill that Rastus would hardly understand that, but then he was too tired to care.

"Greetings, Waa I Saang. I will have you some milk and bread very shortly."

"Just bring it into my room, Rastus; I am very tired."

"Ah, you have had a hard day. You must sleep through the night for a change."

Bill looked at him kindly and said, "Rastus, when you say your prayers tonight, you might mention that to the good Lord. I think it would be fine to sleep all night for a change."

After a big glass of milk and a half-dozen slices of bread with what little canned butter he could spare, Bill stretched out on his small bunk in the Spartan room that he called his own. As he lay there with his head pillowed on his arm, he tried to reach into his feelings to get hold of just what was bothering him. He was not exactly afraid—goodness knows, he had had a lot more to be afraid of many times before—but something made him uneasy.

About three o'clock the next morning, Chinese Communist soldiers brought a dozen young Communist indoctrinated teachers to a small meeting room near the center of Wuchow. There a local People's Republic official briefed them for the responsibility which was theirs that night. They were going to search the head-quarters and arrest Dr. William Wallace, who was "President Truman's chief spy in Wuchow."

"Ai," murmured the teachers. They knew Dr. Wallace. Who would have thought he was a spy? But if the Government said so, alas, it must be so.

Following the revelation of the operation which was to include the arrest of some of the Catholic missionaries in the hills back of Wuchow, the teachers departed with a group of thirty or more Communist soldiers. Silently, they moved up through the mist-shrouded streets of Wuchow to the gates of the clinic of the Stout Memorial Hospital. As the rest of them melted into the shadows along the wall, one rapped on the door and said, "Let us in." They could hear some fumbling inside and then a servant answered, "Who is there?" The leader grinned at his hiding fellows and answered, "We have a sick man here. Open up."

When the gates swung open, the soldiers quickly pushed aside the frightened servant and dispatched themselves throughout the compound according to their assignments. Several soldiers sur-rounded the hospital while others moved to each of the nearby bungalows and wakened the inhabitants. Others went to each of the hospital's floors and rounded up the staff.

In the old Beddoe bungalow where Bill Wallace was getting his few hours of desperately needed sleep, Rastus awoke upon hearing the commotion and ran to the door. As soon as he opened it, three soldiers burst inside and rudely pushed him against the wall. They marched into Bill's room and ordered him from his bed. The dead-panned soldiers then began a hastily conducted search. In their padded uniforms with the soft cap and the red star, there was a kind of a group anonymity about them. It was as if Communist indoctrination had robbed them of any individuality—here was the new "Chinese man."

In a moment, they seemed satisfied and ordered Bill and the servant to the hospital. As they left, Rastus turned to lock the door to the bungalow, but he was roughly prevented from doing so by the official in charge.

When Bill stepped into the light of the fifth-floor room where the staff had been gathered, he was greeted by cries of concern and fear from the staff. They looked to him as children to a father. He quieted them with a word of assurance, and then walking to their front, turned to face his accusers.

The officer in charge of the group, a young man with eyes deep set for a Chinese and obviously an educated man, said to them, "We know this is a den of spies. The People's Republic is aware that some of you are counterrevolutionaries. This will not be tolerated. Dr. Wallace, we know that you are President Truman's chief spy here in South China. You have been found out; you will no longer be able to carry on your clandestine activities."

A gasp of protest arose from the staff. "It is not true . . . Not Waa I Saang . . . No, you are wrong."

"Enough!" The harsh command from the unsmiling leader brought immediate silence. "We shall prove it to you. Either he has deceived you, too, or else," and he narrowed his eyes, "you are a part of his treasonous activities."

"We are what we seem to be." They all turned as Bill spoke in measured tones. "We are doctors and nurses and hospital staff engaged in healing the suffering and sick in the name of Jesus Christ. We are here for no other reason."

"Aha! You speak smoothly, but we expected as much. No matter. We shall see for ourselves the proof."

Looking around the room, he pointed out the hospital evangelist and the business manager and indicated that they should witness the search. Then taking Bill and Rastus with them, the soldiers went downstairs and across to Bill's bungalow.

When they arrived, the soldiers began a search. They went directly to Bill's room and with feigned surprise discovered a package under the doctor's bamboo bed mat. Hastily unwrapping the brown paper, the leader cried out, "Here is proof!" He held a small pistol.

Rastus, crying out in protest, said, "That was not here before."

At this the leader pushed him roughly against the wall, nearly throttling him with his forearm, and threatened him with the butt end of the pistol.

"Do you want a cauliflower head?"

Bill spoke up and said, "That is not my gun. I do not own a gun, and I do not know where that one came from."

The leader grinned at him and then barked orders for the house to be bolted and secured, and for the doctor to be taken back to the hospital office. At the office, they informed Bill that he was under arrest for suspicion of espionage and that he was going to be taken to their headquarters for further questioning. The leader intimated that he knew that there was also wireless equipment around the hospital and that they would search until they found it.

Meanwhile, Everley Hayes had been placed under house arrest and was not allowed to talk to Bill. From her window, she saw the soldiers march Bill off between them for questioning. As they disappeared into the streets of Wuchow, she had the strange feeling that she would never see him again.

Faced with wild charges of espionage and hints of other darker charges to come, Bill was placed in a cell and left alone for some time. He was able to receive meals from the hospital and had an opportunity to tell his jailer of Jesus Christ and to preach from a cell window to two or three peasants who gathered to hear him. When this was reported to the hospital staff, they rejoiced, and

Everley and the hospital administrator made formal requests for the release of the doctor. It was impossible for them to inform either the American consul or the Foreign Mission Board. They could only pray, and that they did.

A week after his arrest, the Communists turned away Rastus when he brought Bill's food one morning. They said he would no longer be able to receive it. That night a called meeting was held at one of the big town halls in Wuchow and all citizens of any importance were commanded to attend. There the man who had arrested the doctor arose to inform the crowd that Dr. William Wallace of the Stout Memorial Hospital had confessed to being a spy and being in the pay of President Truman. They spoke of the gun and hinted at dark deeds the doctor had done. They asked for those who had any accusation against Dr. Wallace to come forward with their charges. None came. When the planted Communist denouncers began to yell vindictive statements against the doctor, they were surprised that the crowd—despite their training—did not join them. No one was deceived; the doctor was being railroaded and everyone knew it.

What the Communists had secured from Bill was a statement concerning his name, age, length of service in China, and other factual matters. Reading it and realizing it was all true, he signed it. The Communists then typed into a blank part of the paper the statement that he had been sent to China as a secret service man by the United States Government. This was the confession.

Next day, Bill was awakened early and shoved out into a court-yard where he realized for the first time he was not the only missionary being held. He recognized a Catholic sister and a bishop. Grinning despite the circumstances, he spoke to them and they greeted each other warmly before they were rudely separated.

Another step was taken in the fiendish Communist conspiracy to discredit the popular doctor. A placard with obscene and derisive accusations and charges was placed over him; his hands were tied behind his back. With others, he was marched through the streets to the Fu River and across to the main prison halfway up the hill— that same hill to which he had gone so many times before for fellowship with his friends, the Christian and Missionary Alliance people. On the way over, shoved by a guard, he fell and badly hurt a hand that he threw out to break his fall. He received no care.

Daily, sometimes hourly, often through the night at the prison, he was awakened and brought to an interrogator's room. The world had yet to hear of brainwashing, which was to be more fully publicized after the release of the prisoners of the Korean War, but Bill Wallace began to experience it the second week of his imprisonment. The singleminded, sensitive young doctor who had dedicated his whole life and being to one thing, to serve the Lord Jesus Christ and his fellowmen through medicine, found that the Communists had conjured a list of crimes that "Dante's demons could not improve upon."

Their accusations, viciously and vehemently proclaimed, bewildered and upset him. They were shouted over and over again, growing in intensity, growing in degradation, allowing for no defense. No excuses or answers were permitted. It overwhelmed him to hear accusations of incompetence in surgery, of murdering and maiming Chinese patients, of performing illegal and obscene operations. His interrogators hinted that doctors from all over China had gathered evidence on him and were demanding his punishment. When exhausted, he was returned to his cell—a bare room with a thin pallet for protection from the damp and cold and filth of the floor.

On another day, all the foreign prisoners were gathered into an open courtyard and one by one forced to stand by a table piled high with guns, bullets, opium, radios, and other items supposed to have been confiscated in the raids in which they were arrested. Then each one was photographed behind the table. When it came Bill's turn to step up to the table, he was almost pushed into it by the guard behind him. Rudely, he was posed, with great stress being put upon his holding the aerial of a radio—to prove the spying charges.

It was obvious to the Catholic missionaries who were in prison with Bill and who were later released, that he was shaken and strained by the ordeal of interrogation. The rest of that day the prisoners were sport for a large crowd of Communist soldiers, men and women, and they suffered all manner of indignities and brutalities. Toward the end of the day, one of the missionaries found an opportunity to inquire of Bill how he was holding out.

Managing a weak grin, he replied, "All right, trusting in the Lord."

Bill Wallace was fighting the battle of his life. The battle was not whether he could out-argue his accusers. He was not even equipped to begin. It was not a battle of physical endurance, though that soon became involved. It was a battle for sanity.

From his cell in the night, Bill sometimes cried out in agony after the battle was over. With pieces of paper and a smuggled pencil, he wrote short affirmations to try to keep his mind centered on things that he could anchor himself to. Some were Scripture passages, others simple denials of guilt, protests of innocence. He stuck these on the walls of his barren room and repeated them to himself in an effort to prepare for the next interrogation.

But each one came like a high wave. At times, he was all but overwhelmed by the interrogation. Delirium, crying, and blank periods came, but he fought on—clinging to his faith. His fellow victims, not yet subjected to the intensive brainwashing, helplessly watched this inhuman assault on one of the greatest men they had ever known. Frantically, they tried to reach him from time to time by calling through their cells. But it was a lonely battle which only Bill and the Lord—who loved him and who, somehow, in his wildest delirium he affirmed—could face.

Then something went wrong. The Communists plainly intended to brainwash their victim into an open confession, to have him repudiate publicly all that he was and all he had stood for. They thought their goal was within reach, but the tough spirit would not capitulate so easily, and his protests rang through the night.

The guards, driven by fear or perhaps guilt, came to his cell in the night with long poles and cruelly thrust them between the cell bars to jab the doctor into unconsciousness. Somebody figured wrong. For one night the battle was over, and, though no one heard Bill Wallace cry, "It is finished," he offered up his spirit and brought his ministry and mission to a close. Quietly, his soul slipped from his torn body and his exhausted mind and went to be with the One he had so faithfully and unstintedly served.

Bill Wallace was dead to the world, but was alive forever with God.

The next morning the guards ran down the cellblock, crying that the doctor had hanged himself. Asking the two Catholic fathers imprisoned in the cell to come with them, they went into the cell where the body of the doctor was hanging from a beam by a rope of braided quilt. The guards tried to get the fathers to sign a statement that he had committed suicide. They would not do so. They finally signed a statement saying how they had found him, but they suspected that the Communists were trying to make a murder look like a suicide.

Back at the hospital where the staff had waited prayerfully through all these weeks, word came to go and get the body of Dr. Wallace. Everley went with her servant and another nurse. They would not let her go into the cell, but they let the servant in, and Everley instructed him quietly to be sure to note the characteristics of the body. The facial characteristics of hanging were missing— bulging eyes, discolored face, swollen tongue. Instead, the upper torso was horribly bruised. The Communists had tried to cover up one botch with another; however, every effort was made to keep the missionary nurse from seeing this.

A cheap wooden coffin had been brought, and as soon as the body was dressed, it was put into the coffin and nailed shut by the Communist soldiers. With the few hospital people who were allowed to come and with the soldiers escorting—or, more accurately, guarding—they set out from Wuchow.

In a small leaking boat, they paddled downriver under bleak February skies until they came to the bamboo-shaded cemetery that clung to the side of the hill overlooking the river. A grave was dug, but no service was allowed, and the Communist soldiers stayed until the last spade of dirt had been put in. Afterward, they drove everyone away, leaving the clod-heaped grave to mark the resting place of one of China's great Christian saints.

As the boats pulled away from the bank, the grieving nurse looked back at the lonely scene, overwhelmed by the seeming abandonment of her fellow worker's final resting place.

It did not remain an unmarked grave for long. Bill's Chinese friends were shocked by the loss of the doctor who had lived only to serve them. No amount of People's propaganda could make them believe he was anything other than what they had known him to be. Despite the danger involved, they collected a fund for a marker and lovingly built a monument over the lonely grave.

They laid a cement terrace on the grave and another on the level below it. Concrete steps led from the lower terrace to the grave. Over it, they erected a single shaft reaching heavenward. On the shaft they inscribed in simple Scripture their estimate of the life of Dr. William L. Wallace:

"For to Me to Live Is Christ"

17

"And to Die Is Gain"

Everley Hayes unfastened her seat belt and reached for her purse. She checked again to see if the little box was in the purse and then looked out the window at the approaching terminal building. Knoxville, Tennessee, was a new town to her, but she felt an undefined nostalgia, as if she had been there before. It seemed strange that this was where Bill Wallace's life began; it seemed stranger that it had ended on the willow-shrouded banks of China's West River.

As the plane taxied toward the gate, she rested her head back against the seat and tried to remember. Like slides clicking in and out a projector, she recalled the scenes the Stegalls would want to hear about: the hospital, the staff, Newbern, Rastus, Bill. . . . She wanted to remember him laughing, making rounds, at the helm of his boat, roughing his beloved German shepherd, Duchess. For a while, especially during the six long months she was interned in Wuchow, all she had remembered was his lean figure being led away into the darkness the night the Communists came, and the cell where they claimed his body. Now she could remember the happier moments; now she could visit the Stegalls.

Sydney and Ruth Lynn Stegall and their son embraced Everley as if she were a member of the family, though it was their first meeting. During the long months since Bill's death, they had prayed for Everley's release and her safe return to the States. Somehow they could not lay their turbulent feelings to rest until they talked to her. There were too many things they had to know.

As Everley walked about the restful, tree-shaded Stegall yard, she remembered the time Bill told her of the place he called his permanent address. She and Bill had walked to the old Christian cemetery after a long surgical stint. They walked up the green hill

152

where vine-covered remains of the Kwangsi War fortifications slowly faded into history. They walked on down a winding green path to the last resting place of the Beddoes' only son, of the Rays' little girl, of the wife of an early missionary, and of several French and German naval men killed in a long-forgotten river incident.

As they took the river path back, Bill talked about home. The brick patio, the barbecue pit, the dogwoods and maples, all were as he had described them. She understood the reason for her undefinable nostalgia. It was the vivid descriptions she had heard from him, giving her the feeling that she had actually been here.

Sydney Stegall interrupted her reverie. "William always slept on that breezeway when he was home on furloughs. He said it was more like home, though he missed his log pillow. One night for a joke I put some bricks under his pillow. The next morning Bill laughingly told me that he had the best night's sleep in weeks."

Everley laughed, "That sounds like him. He needed less to be comfortable than anyone I ever knew."

It was the first time they had mentioned Bill and they all realized it. Ruth Lynn Stegall said, "There is so much we want to know, Everley. So very much."

Everley's eyes were full. "And there's a lot to tell."

After dinner, they settled back to talk. The Stegalls wanted to hear about her release from China first. Everley confessed that the six months between Bill's death and her release were terribly hard.

"I was actually afraid of losing my mind. The Communists would not let me leave my house and yard nor talk to any of the staff. From my window, I could see them passing to and from the hospital, now and then casting fearful glances in my direction. Sometimes I waved, but they seldom dared respond. You never knew who was a spy in your midst during those last months. This was one of the most nerve-racking aspects of the time we were behind the Bamboo Curtain. Bill was philosophical about it when he was alive, but it got under my skin.

"I played my piano and read and re-read a psychiatric textbook I had, in order to keep my attention on anything but Bill's death and my own uncertain future. I prayed and read my Bible and asked God more than once, 'Why?' "

Sydney nodded. "We've asked that one ourselves."

Everley continued, "I applied at least once a week for permission to leave, but all I got was the run-around. Then one day, they told me I had permission, but that I would have to leave within twenty-four hours. Also, I was to take out with me only the bare necessities."

She looked at them apologetically. "I really wanted to bring some of Bill's things, but they confiscated most of them, and I was not allowed to go after the rest."

Ruth Lynn said, "Of course, we understand. We are just glad that you are here."

"I did manage to sneak this out, though." Everley dug the little box from her purse and opened it with care. From it, she extracted a small gold ring and handed it to Ruth Lynn. "This was Bill's chop ring. We took it from his hand. I guess they overlooked it."

"Chop ring?" Ruth Lynn was puzzled by the term.

"It is a Chinese custom. A kind of signature ring. See, these characters stand for his name. In the old days, it was used to press into the wax that was sealing a letter."

"Why is the piece missing?" Sydney fingered the treasure. "Did you have to cut it off?"

"No." Everley smiled. "Bill said he used a piece of it to fill his tooth during the year he was refugeeing in western China."

They were silent for a moment.

"Everley, we believe that somehow God used Bill's death for His glory even as he used his life." Ruth Lynn spoke firmly. "We've heard from so many who have been inspired and encouraged by Bill's dedication that I have come to believe it was a part of God's plan for his life."

Sydney got up and went to a desk. "You ought to read some of the things people have said." Taking a sheaf of letters and clippings he walked to Everley's side. "For instance, listen to this letter from Mr. Newbern." They were quiet as he read.

"Bill's death was more than a shock to us; it left us with a deep sense of loss. But we are also conscious of another deep impression. It is that Bill Wallace was an honored man. We cannot escape the impression that Bill felt he would be called to walk through 'the valley of the shadow of death.' He thought it was God's will. There have been and there will be many martyrs, but few can so glorify Him in death as Bill did."

Sydney continued, "Listen to this letter from a Swedish missionary who is serving in Indonesia now."

"He loved the Chinese enough to give his life for them, and they loved him enough to entrust their lives into his hands. . . . His life has been a challenge to our lives."

Ruth Lynn said, "Read her the one from Dr. Rankin."

Sydney shuffled through the letters and then began reading again. "When God chooses someone to make a superlative witness of his love, he chooses a superlative child of his. He chose his own Son, Jesus, to make the witness on the Cross. And now it seems that he chose Bill to make this witness. To give his life in love and service for the people whom he served fits in naturally and harmoniously with Bill's life. The two things go together because he was that kind of man. His life's service among men bears out the testimony of his death. Bill's death was not the result of his being caught by a situation from which he could not escape. He deliberately chose his course with a committal that made him ready to take any consequences that might come. He followed the same course when the Japanese armies approached Wuchow and he has followed it throughout his missionary service."

"Here is a statement from Dr. Cauthen." Sydney handed the clipping to Everley and she read her area secretary's words.

"Many things about the death of Bill Wallace make us think of the death of the Christ. The authorities were envious of his place in the hearts of people. They used falsehood in order to bring charges against him. They tried to represent him as an agent of the American Government, as the Jews tried to represent Jesus as one stirring up revolt against Rome. They sought to stir up public sentiment by calling large groups of people together. They subjected him to a bitter and cruel imprisonment. Early in his imprisonment it was reported he was required to empty toilet buckets and do other such tasks.

"Just as in the case of Jesus the enemies of the truth sought to discredit his testimony by declaring the disciples had come and stolen away his body, so in Wuchow the Communists stated that Dr. Wallace had died by strangling himself. This nobody believes even a moment. It is obviously an effort on the part of Communists both to discredit his testimony and to leave themselves free from the charge of having taken his life. . . .

"In the death of Bill Wallace, communism reveals its real character as a movement undertaking to destroy that which Christ stands for. As it exerts its energy against the people of Christ, however, it will be repeatedly made evident that Christ's people are willing to do for the Lord today as they have been throughout the ages."

When she finished, Sydney, holding another article, said, "A doctor voiced my own feelings, though. This came from the Journal of the International College of Surgeons." He read the clipping:

"Such men as this are the soul of the college; in their humility no less than in their strengths lies the embodiment of the ideals that beckon us all. . . . The Chinese Communist Party, in its valiant efforts to remake the world, found Bill Wallace's presence in China an inconvenience. He was a living example of all they abhorred. More than that, he had an influence, quiet as he was. No selfless life is devoid of effects upon others."

Sydney took his glasses off and looked at his wife, then at the nurse who had served alongside his beloved brother-in-law. "From what we are constantly hearing, we know that William's life is going to continue to mean much to the kingdom of God. I believe he is going to mean even more in ways we will never hear about. I refuse to count his life a tragedy; it was a beautiful life lived with a magnificent purpose that was and is being realized."

Everley's eyes were moist. "I keep remembering the Scripture verse they put on his grave, 'For to me to live is Christ.' The rest of the Scripture passage says, 'and to die is gain'."

Epilogue

This is the story of the life and death of Dr. William L. Wallace of Knoxville, Tennessee, and Wuchow, China. A fire that blazed so high is bound to have an afterglow; the afterglow of Bill Wallace's life is still bright, more than ten years later.

It's bright in Knoxville where the lovely Wallace Memorial Church has over a thousand members and is still growing. It is remembered and honored through the memorial educational building of his own church, Broadway Baptist.

In Little Rock, Arkansas, the Baptist students of the University School of Medicine worship in a chapel named for Bill Wallace. And in the little town of Indio, California, a church named for the missionary doctor continues to pursue its own witness in the same unselfish manner.

A section of the medical school library where he studied is dedicated to him, a reminder to doctors-in-the-making of one who is a part of their heritage.

In the midst of the suffering and need in Pusan, Korea, stands one of the most significant memorials of all, the Wallace Memorial Baptist Hospital. Here, missionary doctors, inspired by Bill's life, minister in the same spirit. The hospital was founded by Bill's old colleague, Rex Ray. And the first head nurse in the strategic institution was none other than Lucy Wright, who had served with Bill Wallace in the hospital in the wilderness.

Everley Hayes is serving in Indonesia now. She is head nurse in the Baptist hospital on the island of Java, where Bill Wallace used to say he would like to begin medical work if they ever got out.

157